ART AND SOUL

ART AND SOUL

HOWARD MCCONEGHEY

FOREWORD BY THOMAS MOORE

SPRING PUBLICATIONS, INC.
PUTNAM, CONNECTICUT

Classics in Archetypal Psychology 7

Copyright © 2003 by Spring Publications, Inc.
All rights reserved.
"Foreword," © 2003 by Thomas Moore.

Cover design: Sandy Gellis and Margot McLean.
Cover image: Charles Demuth, detail of
"Eggplant and Tomatoes," watercolor, 1926.
Collection of James and Barbara Palmer, State College, PA.
Printed in Canada—text on acid-free paper.

Distributed in the United States by the Continuum
Publishing Group; in the United Kingdom,
Eire and Europe by Airlift Book Co.

First Edition

Library of Congress Control Number:
2003102926

ISBN 0-88214-383-2

SPRING PUBLICATIONS, INC.
28 Front St. Suite 3, Putnam, CT 06260
tel 860 963-1191 fax 860 963-1826

springpublications@hotmail.com
www.springpub.com
secure online bookstore

CONTENTS

FOREWORD
by Thomas Moore
i

INTRODUCTION
v

I AESTHETIC PERCEPTION
1

II GIVE FORM
23

III WORK FOR CLARITY
39

IV CARE ENOUGH
55

V NEVER GENERALIZE
69

VI STICK TO THE IMAGE
83

LIST OF ILLUSTRATIONS

Figure 1: *Eggplant and Tomatoes,* Charles Demuth.
Collection James and Barbara Palmer. State College, PA.

Figure 2: *Rolling Power,* Charles Sheeler.
Smith College Museum of Art, Northampton, MA.

Figure 3: *Still Life with Kitchen Utensils,* Jean-Baptiste Simeon Chardin.
Ashmolean Museum, Oxford.

Figure 4: *Kitchen Table,* Jean-Baptiste Simeon Chardin.
Museum of Fine Arts, Boston, MA.

Figure 5: *The Scream,* Edvard Munch.
National Gallery of Art, Washington, DC.

Figure 6: *The Scream* (with axes), Edvard Munch.
National Gallery of Art, Washington, DC.

Figure 7: *Home,* Art Therapy Client.

Figure 8: *Home* (with axes), Art Therapy Client.

Figure 9: *Christ,* Child's Drawing.

Figure 10: *Head of Christ,* Georges Rouault.
Chrysler Museum of Art, Norfolk, VA.

Figure 11: *Christ,* Child's Drawing.

Figure 12: *Christ,* Child's Drawing.

Figure 13: *Christ,* Child's Drawing.

Figure 14: *Crucifix,* Anon. Taylor Museum
Fine Arts Center, Colorado Springs, CO.

Figure 15: *Christ,* Child's Drawing.

Figure 16: *Penitente Nazarene Christ,* Anon. Taylor Museum
Fine Arts Center, Colorado Springs, CO.

Figure 17: *Bleeding Hands of Christ,* Student Drawing
(With permission).

Figure 18: *Bleeding Hand,* Student Drawing
(With permission).

Figure 19: *Bleeding Hand* (enlarged), Student Drawing
(With permission).

Figure 20: *Bleeding Hand* (final drawing), Student Drawing
(With permission).

Figure 21: *Hand with Pencil,* Student Drawing
(With permission).

Figure 22: *Les Mains,* Fernand Léger.
Galerie Jeanne Bucher, Paris.

Figure 23: *Hand with Wheat,* Student Drawing
(With permission).

FOREWORD

We have not yet rediscovered the place of art in human life. We still marginalize artists, treat works of art as financial commodities and objects of moral scrutiny, and fail to support art in our schools. I say rediscover because once, before our infatuation with technology and science, we understood the role of art in religion, public life, and individual psychology. We knew that compared to endless studies and research programs, art was a more precise and effective way of conjuring the mysteries that define our lives. But in a relatively short time, we have been seduced away from art by the cool devotees of the machine, and this neglect of art not insignificantly has gone on hand in hand with a cultural loss of soul.

Howard McConeghey understands this situation fully, much more intimately than I do, and he has spent a lifetime doing what I consider to be one of the key tasks of any culture—teaching art. I have known students of his for many years and have seen the remarkable ways they approach art and bring it into the center of life. I have also witnessed their understanding of the depth and mystery of the images they work with and make. They know the difference between an image that breathes life and a nice picture of something. They also can distinguish between self-expression as ego-centered, revolving around the self, and as the manifestation of soul.

For before all else Howard is a soul-maker. For him art is a way of life. He lives his creativity; he doesn't merely express it. His home and studio are the incarnation of Renaissance ideals of a culture of images transforming practical space into the dreamscape of soul. He is a constant and faithful artist. There is no on-off switch in him to separate his life in art from his life as a whole. In his being he manifests the ideal intimacy between soul and art, and so we all have much to learn from him. Knowing this secret of Howard's nature, for years I have hoped that he would complete this book. I go into art galleries today and see ideology, technique, and self-expression everywhere. I see the trickery of clever methods and ideas. Rarely do I sense the shamanic essence of the artist. The capacity to shut down usual modes of thinking—we can all think when we have to—and allow images and mysteries to appear and then find manifestation in precise and original color, line, and texture. Philosopher and critic George Steiner distinguishes between novelty and originality in art. Novelty is the appearance of something apparently new, while originality in art is a return of and to origins. Aesthetic inventions are archaic, he says.

Howard uses a related term that he gets from James Hillman—archetypal. The word means "original impression," a good description of Howard's approach to art and art education. To him art gives presence to the timeless realities of soul within the context of current life, fully and individually lived.

Because we live in a time when, as Howard says again and again, we look for literal and pragmatic solutions to problems, art therapy and art education turn toward the literal and the pragmatic in specific ways. Therapists sometimes use art for facile diagnosis and treatment.

They assume that images betray symbolically and in shorthand emotions and fantasies that the person is not aware of. The watchful therapist catches these slips of tongue and of the painter's hand and exploits them for the therapeutic project. A much more subtle approach would treat art as imagistic, full of mystery, and impossible to translate into simple explanation. The therapeutic dimension might be nothing more than a deepening of the life in a person as manifested in imagistic presentations of soul. In the best art therapy, the status of the artist would not be compromised—a person would be a therapist and a real artist at the same time.

Howard explores these issues with steadied, delicate attention to soul in art. At the same time he deepens the very notion of therapy so that eventually art and therapy meet at a place where they are both intact. The same subtlety applies to art education, where artistic expression cannot be separated from the artist's being and the deep well from which images arise.

A culture can be measured by its art. If our culture is full of ideology and personal cleverness, this situation merely reflects values in the culture as a whole. On the other hand, by getting our art in place along the lines Howard McConeghey sketches out in this book, we might find our way toward a cultural renewal. Art is also the forerunner of cultural change because it so profoundly affects the imagination that shapes our vision. Art is a kind of philosophy, not the abstract kind of the schools, but the life-and-blood philosophy carved out and painted by the artist whose materials and tools are essentially alchemical instruments used primarily for the education of soul.

Philosophy is a lived thing, the imagination of our lives that permeates every moment and every act. What Howard has given us in this remarkable book is a philosophy of art that doesn't get lost in abstractions the way much aesthetic theory does. These are the reflections not only of a working artist, but a thoughtful, devoted alchemist. Jung showed us that alchemy is the primary dynamic of soul. It was called the Art with a capital "A," and when our artists discover that their work is first the alchemical revelation of soul, then their art and the ancient and timeless Art of soul might overlap, and we will have found what all that mixing of color and distortion of realistic form is all about.

In the end art education is a mystery. I don't know of any teacher or any writing that presents this mysterious work with the knowing skill and subtle insight of Howard McConeghey in this manifesto for a new yet ancient way of approaching apprenticeship in the realm of art. I would like to see this book become a school and a movement, not in a rigid, literal sense but as a serious, widely accepted way of doing and teaching art in our institutions. Art therapy needs redefinition along these lines, and art education has yet to discover the heart of its work.

When I was studying religion at Syracuse University twenty-five years ago, I recall many students in literature and art taking courses in our department. There they could study images in depth, while in their own departments the emphasis was on technicalities and vocabularies, the developmental history of their arts, and schools and theories. In Howard's work I see the reconciliation of these two approaches, or the taking back into art a concern for depth, ultimate seriousness, and relevance in the most profound sense of the word.

For all its play and imagination, nothing is more important to the lives of us all than art. It is the only thing that speaks directly to soul, unless you would consider religion, which, when understood as an affair of soul, is inseparable from art—art and religion are simply two sides of a coin. Howard's book is not just a new theory about art or an application of archetypal psychology to art education. It is a complete vision of life, rooted in soul, that teaches each of us, whatever mode of image-work we might prefer, how to craft a life with soul.

—Thomas Moore

INTRODUCTION

Art education in public school curriculae has been supported because it can develop good taste and assure a supply of commercial and industrial designers. But aesthetic education can help a student develop a sense of reality and cope with it, for "...art is a way of coming to terms with experience."[1] During my years of teaching art, I learned that art classes do more than train artists. They can lead students to an appreciation of the living God within. It develops the imagination and opens eyes to the necessity of beauty. It is primarily for this reason that the practice of art therapy grew out of art education. Its pioneers, like me, were educators and art teachers.

However the language of clinical psychotherapy and academic aesthetics—based as they are on concepts of external behavior, analysis and development—was not acceptable as a foundation for the kind of art therapy or art education I wanted to build. Instead I looked to archetypal psychology and phenomenological philosophy to develop a solid aesthetic position. This was a necessary step: unlike other psychologies, archetypal psychology proclaimed the importance of art and provided an authoritative language for art educators and therapists, while phenomenological philosophers, such as Martin Heidegger, offered ideological support.

This book was written with the help and influence of various scholars who have moved my thoughts about the essential nature of art in therapy and education. It is loosely structured around five basic principles drawn from my experience as an art educator and an art

---

[1] Seonaid M. Robertson, *Rosegarden and Labyrinth* (Dallas: Spring Publications, 1989), 107.

therapist. This is a simple attempt to situate these ideas within the psyche and to emphasize the importance of imagination as the basis of human thought and action.

Art has too long been subservient to scientific professions such as medicine and education. Yet art's authority in the theater of emotions is important. Art-making is a way of ordering the self. Art can teach us how to face rages, fears, and passions and to see these as universal feelings. Emotions come to us from somewhere other than the self. Poet William Blake, seeing that emotions originate outside of human control, called emotions divine influxes. Art is a language which allows us to speak to these divine influxes. Art-making teaches us imagination, perhaps giving us access to the divine forces Blake spoke of and helping us to give them meaningful order. James Hillman, founder of archetypal psychology, puts it succinctly: "Restoration of the imagination is the fundamental cure of disordered emotion, and especially the imagination that gives place to the more-than-human."[2]

There has recently been an effort in art therapy circles to find an authoritative language appropriate to our specific *métier*. The ideas we find in Hillman's "new spirit of psychology" and in phenomenological philosophy offers the most meaningful speech and manner of thinking for art therapy and art education. These sources speak to our professions with depth and offer a new spirit of aesthetic perception. Their aptness for art education and art therapy resides chiefly in the appreciation that the psyche is autonomous, and that the speech of psyche is always presented in images. Many of us have lost the ability to see this. Joseph Campbell, a mythologist well versed in the ideas of analytical psychology, argued that even contemporary poets and artists are lost. "They are at sea because the traditions don't tell them that their inspirations come from divine transcendent sources... They think studio problems are what it's all about..."[3]

This book includes both art education and art therapy—and often speaks of them as one and the same—because both claim art as their *modus operandi* and both speak of the art of children and the general public. The two fields serve the entire populace, not only the talented

[2] James Hillman, *Emotion* (Evanston, Ill.: Northwestern UP, 1992), xv.
[3] Joseph Campbell, *This Business of the Gods* (Caledon East Ontario, Canada: Windrose Films Ltd. 1989), 120.

few who pursue art as a profession. And when I speak of art education in this book, I speak of art education as taught in elementary and secondary schools, not the education of artists in professional schools and academies.

Many of the ideas in this book are borne out of experience. Like many of my colleagues, I came to art therapy via art education, which I practiced at all levels from preschool through graduate programs for forty years. I founded the art therapy program at the University of New Mexico in 1975 and directed it until my retirement in 1990.

I am indebted to many people, and I am deeply grateful to all those who have influenced my thinking over the years. My wife, Evelyn, has read the manuscript and has been helpful throughout the writing. I have learned much from my students and art therapy patients, and I am deeply indebted to the University of New Mexico for granting me a sabbatical in 1987 to work on this book; especially to Dean David Darling of the College of Education who encouraged me in the establishment of an archetypal art therapy program as a part of the Department of Art Education, and to his successor, Dean David Colton whose warm support and scholarly interest were an inspiration to me. There are so many influences from my earliest interest in art and art education to the present that I hardly know where to stop, but the list would be too long. Early art teachers whose influence has been strong and lasting were Illa Mae Talley, Mildred Cunningham, and John Horns. John was my true mentor and faithful friend for as long as he lived. The late Eleanor Ulman, founder and long time editor of *The American Journal of Art Therapy*, who was prominent in the American Art Therapy Association in the early days, offered friendly and helpful advice for getting an art therapy program started at U. N. M., and Vija Lusebrink, art therapy professor at the University of Louisville, provided much needed reassurance which gave me the courage to focus our program boldly and directly on archetypal psychology. Shaun McNiff, who founded the art therapy program at Lesley College, has given warm and friendly support for archetypal ideas and for our program. Ethne Gray, Jungian analyst and art therapist, has encouraged the National Association to acknowledge Jungian and archetypal art therapy. She and I organized the National Conference of Jungian Art Therapists, and she edits, IRIS, its newsletter. Ethne read the first two chapters of this book and made helpful suggestions. David Maclagan, a British art therapist, read the first chapter and made suggestions which have been useful throughout the entire book. Dan Noel read the entire manuscript and gave useful advise. I owe much to Russell Lockhart, friend and analyst whose work and person have been a real inspiration. And finally it was Thomas Moore who urged me to take up the work again after a decade of neglect. I am grateful for his foreword.

Obviously, I owe a huge debt of gratitude to my friend James Hillman, whose work, even though its theme is psychology, articulates more clearly than I could ideas about art and the imagination. Assimilating and teaching Hillman's ideas as they apply to art therapy enriched the last fifteen years of my teaching career and made these years more stimulating, exciting, and challenging than ever.

—Albuquerque, New Mexico, 2000

I

AESTHETIC PERCEPTION

Though it is hidden in all things,
that self shines forth.
Yet it is seen by subtle seers
of superior, subtle intellect.

—Katha Upanisad

The world, the gods, man, and all things have to be looked
upon with a new eye—but looked upon; not shunned.

—Joseph Campbell

The pragmatic outlook, linked as it is with natural science,
holds such sway over us that no academic discussion can
resist its magnetic orienting concepts; its basic
psychologism underlies every doctrine that really looks
respectable.

—Susanne K. Langer

Aesthetic perception is the speech of soul. It is itself an art which is distinct from a rational, pragmatic outlook. To the Greeks the word "aesthetic" meant simply to "to perceive." To perceive means to discern, detect, recognize, apprehend, distinguish, see, appreciate, and decipher, but to perceive aesthetically is to look at the world with "a new eye." Aesthetic perception detects the numinous, what is more than merely physical in the objects we see. It apprehends the *anima mundi* in the ordinary things and experiences of our daily lives.

The term "aesthetic perception" revises the customary sense of the visual to suggest psychological insight and the notion of perception as poetic imagination. Aesthetic perception has little to do with the physical mechanics of sight. Use of the term follows in the footsteps of the poet Percy Bysshe Shelley, who wrote of the dominance of the external world over that of the internal world:

> The cultivation of those sciences which have enlarged the
> limits of the empire of man over the external world, has,
> for the want of the poetical faculty, proportionately cir-
> cumscribed those of the internal world, and man, having
> enslaved the elements, remains himself a slave.[1]

Aesthetic perception, then, is concerned with this poetic faculty which can be seen as psychological since we see the world as much through unconscious images of reality as through the biochemical process of optical sight.

The term the Greeks used for perception, *aesthesis*, can be translated as "taking in," "breathing in," and "a gasp." "Taking in" the world was viewed as a primary response, and this response was considered more than mere visual perception. In a way we have inherited this view. Even our logical thinking must pass through a kind of psychological lens. Once passed through this lens even the mundane becomes imagistic. The modern pragmatic view is itself based upon a particular image of reality. But often the modern definition of perception ignores other possible views and disparages them. Nonetheless our perception of the world is often realized by taking it into ourselves, in the Greek sense of the word, even if we are unaware of how we unconsciously participate with the psyche in the creation of our images of reality.

The "New Eye" and a Break with Scientific Knowing

In order to shed modern—and often limited—ideas of perception, one must begin to see with this "new eye." Developing this new way of looking requires a break with the commonly accepted mode of approaching knowledge; the logical, positivist idea of reality. Here

---

[1] Percy Bysshe Shelley, "A Defense of Poetry" *English Romantic Writers*, David Perkins, ed. (New York: Harcourt Brace Janovich, 1967), 1084.

rational cognition can no longer be the only measure of truth and reality, for imagination, too, is real. Aesthetic perception, the poetic faculty we are seeking, can never be encompassed by rational cognition because it acknowledges that images are both psychological and real.

The pragmatic view which dominates our thinking brings with it the empiricist's ideals of observation, analysis, and verification because it has grown up under the mentorship of natural science, according to Susanne Langer, author of *Feeling and Form*. "The chief assumption that determines the entire procedure of pragmatic philosophy is that all human interests are direct or oblique manifestations of 'drives' motivated by animal needs."[2] Often overriding anything but these animal needs is the reliance on science and its claim on knowledge. Douglas Sloan, a writer who has explored education and forms of learning, has outlined some of the assumptions that limit our ability to see with the "new eye."

> The dominant modern view of how we know, of what we can know, has been shaped by the positivist assumption (in its various modern forms) that all knowledge is acquired only through "the positive data of science" which has meant, in effect, only through that which can be counted, measured, and weighed.[3]

These assumptions which have shaped human thinking and the world that has emerged in the scientific era he calls "the onlooker conscious" or "detached objective observation." This consciousness is comprised of "the view that the whole can be understood in terms of its parts," a form of analysis, and "the premise that reality is basically quantitative" which is verification by counting and measuring.[4]

Philosophers have also tried to define scientific knowing and its effects on perception, and many have come to see its limitations. Martin Heidegger concluded that scientific knowing is not only limited but it drives out every other theory of what is real.[5] Science's pragmatism

---

[2] Susanne Langer. *Feeling and Form* (New York: Charles Scribner's Sons, 1953), 35.

[3] Douglas Sloan, "Toward an Education for Living," Teachers College Record, Vol. 84 no. 1 (New York: 1982), 2.

[4] Douglas Sloan, "Education for a Living World," *Nuclear Reactions* (Albuquerque: Image Press, 1984), 19.

[5] Martin Heidegger, *The Question Concerning Technology and Other Essays*, William Lovitt, trans. (New York: Harper and Row, 1977), 27.

does not allow consideration of the numinous—or aesthetic perception. This is in part because the pragmatic approach is an "either/or" attitude toward reality, while aesthetic perception is a "both/and" attitude; a paradoxical phenomenon. Even hard science has had to deal with this paradox on some level: twentieth-century physicists learned the lesson when light was proven to be both a wave and a particle. It could be said that the wave/particle duality should have marked the end of the "either/or" way of looking at the world because physicists no longer could accept the proposition that light is "either" a particle "or" a wave. But the pragmatic outlook still dominates our culture.

Why does science's pragmatic view have such a tenacious hold on Western consciousness? It may be because its development was necessary. Owen Barfield, in his book *Saving Appearances: A Study in Idolatry*, speculates that this preoccupation with phenomena existing independently from human consciousness—which in its extreme form he has called idolatry—may have been necessary to further the development of consciousness. This would make it a necessary step toward achievement of what he calls "final participation." This final act would coincide with aesthetic perception.[6]

In aesthetic perception the light by means of which we see is that "spark from the generative psyche," and psyche is characterized by beauty. Without the numinous and mysterious we can only think of the world as atomic particles, and the human being is reduced, by pragmatists such as John Dewey, to "the live creature." Dewey and others have relegated the motivations of human beings to the narrow and one-dimensional plane of "animal drives." For science the particularity of each individual object or event is seen as chaos and therefore must be rigorously classified by conscious decision. When conscious decision is thought of as existing within the skin or head of each individual, a collective consciousness cannot be considered. Other claims—like those of Barfield—put our mode of thinking into the role of shaping the phenomenal word and our attitudes towards it.

Since aesthetic perception views psychology as the study of soul (*psyche-logos*), the "new eye" is given back the intuitive power of perception without needing a metaphysical presupposition. With soul as

---

[6] Owen Barfield, *Saving the Appearances: A Study in Idolatry* (New York: Harcourt Brace Janovich, n.d.), 146-47.

mediator, spirit is tied to matter and matter is infused with a spiritual reality. Thus the imagination makes images, not the empirical senses. What the "new eye" sees may not make sense in the literal, scientific world because we perceive images prior to our rational concepts. With aesthetic perception, we may close our eyes in order to "see" the image.

Perception is a reflex like breathing, a sensitive response that can change mere events into meaningful experiences by revealing their import. Aesthetic perception originates on a primordial level of consciousness, a level Sigmund Freud and C. G. Jung called the unconscious. And while we may not always have a grasp of the images the unconscious offers, it is here that aesthetic perception gains its insight. According to Jung, "we cannot know better than the unconscious and its intimations," and in the unconscious world there is "a fair chance of finding what we seek in vain in the conscious world. Where else could it be."[7] It will be our task here to stop seeking in vain in the conscious world and begin to access the images available to us in the unconscious world. The foundation of aesthetic perception is thus psychological and poetical.

But aesthetic perception requires an imaginal psychology. Archetypal psychology—sometimes referred to as a branch of depth psychology—seems to be best suited to aesthetic perception. Founded upon the psychological image—those archetypal patterns of human experience which are displayed in myths and tales—archetypal psychology is firmly seated within the culture of Western imagination, arts, and ideas. Like aesthetic perception, archetypal psychology places primacy on soul and accesses the depths of the unconscious through images. Often these images are presented by myths and dreams. For these reasons archetypal psychology is well suited to the professions of art therapy and art education.

Aesthetic perception has at its core a paradigm of beauty. Western myth offers images of beauty in the forms of gods and goddesses: Aphrodite, goddess of Love and Beauty, and of Psyche, a mortal whose beauty rivaled that of Aphrodite. "The soul is born in beauty," says Hillman, "and feeds on beauty, requires beauty

---

[7] C. G. Jung, *Selected letters of C. G. Jung: 1909 to 1961*, Gerhard Adler and Aniela Jaffé, eds., R. F. C. Hull, trans. (Princeton. Bollingen Series, Princeton UP, 1984), 196.

for its life."[8] To overlook the natural beauty of the soul's speech by turning exclusively to empirical analysis and morality is to expel soul from art therapy and art education. Aesthetic perception aims to correct that oversight and to return imagination and soul—and therefore, beauty—to our work.

Beauty

In seeing beauty one sees imperceptible virtues such as love, temperance, and justice in everyday objects and experiences making these visible in our art work is our goal. But beauty is much more than that which is pleasing to the eye, according to Heidegger:

> Beauty is a fateful gift of the essence of truth, and here truth means the disclosure of what keeps itself concealed. The beautiful is not what pleases, but what falls within that fateful gift of truth which comes to be when that which is eternally nonapparent and therefore invisible attains its most radiantly apparent appearance.[9]

Therefore to embody the image in the materials of art, to make visible that invisible image, is the object of art in both art education and art therapy. To achieve such an objective is in itself beautiful. Hillman writes:

> Beauty is the manifest *anima mundi*—and do notice here it is neither transcendent to the manifest or hiddenly immanent within, but refers to appearances as such, created as they are, in the forms which they are given, sense data, bare facts, Venus Nudata. Aphrodite's beauty refers to the luster of each particular event—its clarity, its particular brightness: that particular things appear at all and in the form in which they appear.[10]

When we speak of beauty in this way, we must ask different questions: Is the work of children and untutored adults who "can't draw a straight line," beautiful? Is it art? Children see more than a likeness in the things they perceive. They create works of art which give form to

---

[8] James Hillman, *The Thought of the Heart and the Soul of the World* (Dallas: Spring Publications, 1992), 39.

[9] Martin Heidegger, *What Is Called Thinking?* (New York: Harper and Row, 1968), 19.

[10] James Hillman, *The Thought of the Heart and the Soul of the World*, 43.

an image rather than mere representations of the physical world. They see a deeper truth, the golden luster of essential reality, the object's direct evocation of its being. The artwork of children often touches the soul with the beauty of the gods seen in the ordinary things they encounter. Beauty is the revelatory manifestation of the essential reality beneath the objective materiality of things.

Aesthetic perception—like Psyche's myth—begins with this idea of beauty and recognizes the deeper beauty which is psyche or soul. We tend to think of beauty only in terms of pleasure and harmony, but this ignores the presence of soul. There is great pain and grief in such a paradigm of beauty because it excludes the breadth of human experience. In contrast aesthetic perception sees beauty in the disagreeable and harsh as well as in the pretty and harmonious. If the presence of psyche suggests a deeper beauty, then beauty must mean participation in the soul of the world, even in the world's grief-filled and wretched moments. Myth does not overlook this: the handmaidens of Aphrodite were Trouble and Sorrow. To participate in the experience of the world means to respond aesthetically. For art therapists and teachers, it means to perceive the aesthetic quality in the artwork of our patients and students.

Too often art educators and art therapists fail to hear Psyche's voice in the modest artwork of their patients and students. Educators and therapists tend to lead patients and students toward purely conventional shapes and ideas, promoting developmental stages and academic principles of art. Many art therapists and educators fail to recognize that it is through the psychological process of aesthetic perception that students can learn and patients can gain health. As art educators and art therapists, we must acknowledge the reality of the imaginal world, and we must realize that the real world of our patients or students can never be reduced solely to empirical data, no matter how extensive that collection of data may be.

Making art with the help of Psyche's voice turns art-making into a psychic—or one could say soulful—event. Children's spontaneous expressions are works of art because they are expressions of psychic events—or perhaps because their art-making is a psychic event. In the world of active imagination (not an imaginary world), the images that appear are not made up. Rather they are real figures who are messengers from the objective psyche. Active imagination is not an arbitrary, exotic, or lyrical construction which arrests or ignores reality. Imagination is an organ of knowledge just as real as the physical sense organs of the body. Imagination reverts outer perceptions to the primordial—or archetypal—images which are paradigmatic of human behavior. Therefore aesthetic perception is not merely a product of sense data even though it may produce a visual configuration. Instead it is the apprehension of the numinous in the things we see and experience.

Henry Schaefer-Simmern is perhaps the single writer on art education and art therapy who clearly stresses this point. He writes:

> A work of art can be distinguished from any other pictorial production by a functional interrelationship of all its parts... This visual configuration may be considered the result of an autonomous mental activity; a mental digestion and transformation of sensory experience into a newly created visual entity. It should be emphasized...that this activity is independent of conceptual intellectual calculation and that it takes place solely within the realm of visual experience.[11]

This activity takes place as a poetic or psychological experience—in the realm of aesthetic perception.

Aesthetic perception recognizes a living essence in all sensory experience. Our participation in this poetic thinking is, as Schaefer-Simmern says, independent of conceptual, intellectual calculation. It is a preformation of the intellectual concept into poetic form which expresses its vital living reality. When Charles Demuth sees a tomato and an eggplant (**fig. 1**), they are more than biological specimens; when Charles Sheeler sees the "Rolling Power" (**fig. 2**) of a steam locomotive, it is more than a mechanical reality. These artists recognize Aphrodite— the numinous or divine—in the ordinary things of daily experience, even our most banal moments. Thus aesthetic perception can be seen as visionary intuition. Aesthetic perception does not construct something unreal. It unveils to our ordinary sight the hidden reality of primordial, essential truth, as in a bunch of vegetables or a train engine.

---

[11] Henry Schafer-Simmern, *The Unfolding of Artistic Activity* (Berkeley: University of California Press, 1961), 8.

The unrepresented background of our perceptions is aesthetic depth—the soul's annunciation of itself in all things. This idea is predicated upon the belief that the most basic reality is invisible and nonphysical. Perceiving it requires a subtle intellect and imaginal thinking. We can only approach the unrepresented background of our perceptions through symbolic thinking.

Symbol must be differentiated from allegory. Allegory is a conceptual operation, implying no transition either to a new plane of being or to a new depth of consciousness. It is a figuration at an identical level of consciousness of what might be known in a different way. Symbol, on the other hand, announces a plane of consciousness distinct from that of rational evidence. It is a cipher of a mystery. Symbol is the only means of saying things which cannot be apprehended in any other way. A pragmatic pursuit of beauty through allegory would be both materialistic and narcissistic—art as a substitute for the "real" thing (i.e., mere representation or as the sublimation of unsociable animal drives). Such allegorizing denies the spiritual necessity of psychic reality. It denies the human hunger for beauty. Allegory is a way of denying the odd, even pathological, nature of psychic images. It looks upon images with amusement or curiosity, rendering them impotent of any therapeutic or educational quality. By looking at psychic images as a moralizing fable or pleasing euphemism, we are distancing ourselves from them and thus weakening their emotional effect. Allegory is a defensive reaction of the rational mind against the power of the soul's irrational imagining, a way of avoiding the emotional impact of aesthetic perception.

As art therapists—and as art teachers as well—we are *theapeutes* in the service of Aphrodite. Like Psyche we cannot escape the difficulties and trials imposed on us by the gods and goddesses, and as therapists and educators our task of image-work is a demanding one. When the "meaning" of a student's or patient's artwork seems perfectly clear to us, and there is no mystery, we may be sure that either we are not recognizing the goddess in the image, or else the patient or student is resisting the imagination and covering up with trivial, conventional figures and patterns. The use of banal or stereotypical patterns is an attempt to evade the demands of Aphrodite, the artistic imperative of psyche.

Original ideas are individualized in a psychic vision, undemonstrable except through embodiment in the artwork itself. Art is an incarnation of the imagination. It gives body to symbolic reality, and we cannot penetrate this imaginal universe with rational abstractions or empirical analysis and measurement. In direct contrast to the empiricist's belief that all knowledge comes from the senses, aesthetic perception is not only based on the conviction that image precedes sensual experience but largely determines it. So-called objective reality is, in fact, only what our image of reality will permit us to see.

Of course an image is not always visual: ideas, too, are images. The Greek root of our word "idea" is *eidos* whose meaning encompasses both that which we see and that by means of which we see. Thus an idea can be seen as not only a concept or logical construct. It can also be seen as an image. This is the paradox in aesthetic perception. If we can know through the image, which is not only what we perceive with our eyes but is the source of our ability to see, then the image itself is invisible to the physical eye. In other words it is a psychological reality seen by the eyes of the soul.

The picture, the movement, poem, tune, gesture are the incarnation of the image. Without such embodiment these expressions would remain nothing more than a potentiality. The rolling power of Sheeler's locomotive (**fig. 2**), the slimy posts and mossy bricks of Constable's mills, the serenity of Cezanne's stately mountain are each the embodiment of a poetic image. Art therapy and art education become consequential in the light of this act of incarnating the image. Or, one might say, consequence lies in crafting the images into objects in our world. But the embodiment of the image is not necessarily complete when the painting is painted or the poem written. Its completion depends upon communication. Here lies the role for the art teacher and the art therapist: the image is complete when we respond to the work.

Mnemosyne, the Greek goddess of memory, is the foundation of this communication. "Mnemosyne is the mother of the muses who gives birth to spontaneous speech, song, art, dance, poetry, and other manifestations rendering the numinous visual and experiential."[12] In

---

[12] Russell Lockhart, *Psyche Speaks: A Jungian Approach to Self and World* (Willmette, Ill.: Chiron Publications, 1987), 55-56.

this way Mnemosyne is not just spoken of and about but enacted. In service to Mnemosyne we each become tellers and doers in relation to what we experience, and therapists and teachers can provide perceptive feedback. This is the direction which art educators and art therapists can follow. It is the manifestation of aesthetic perception.

Connecting with the spontaneous images of the psyche is essential for the ailing world as well as for the individual. We often fail to realize that such individual work is critical for everyone.

> If we lose connection with the living blood of the psyche…we will come to know that state so devastatingly pictured by Orozco in his Dartmouth College mural of "The Gods of the Modern World" where "the dead give birth to dead things."[13]

If we follow this line of thinking, the image-work of the individual is crucial to the life of our gasping culture, and art therapy and art education are given a new and powerful tool.

Nurturing the Image

Traditional art education is based on training talented people. But art-making is important for everyone, whether they are talented or not, because art encourages that poetic process which gives life to spontaneous aesthetic impulses. Those who are interested in the service of psyche—both the personal psyche and the *anima mundi*—see art as a correspondence with soul. When art education sees art this way, it is not far from art therapy which also sees the importance of art and image for everyone, especially those who are psychologically restless or disturbed. The lines between the two professions become blurred: without that spark from the generative psyche, there can be no therapy, no learning, and no art. Such nurturing of the image is necessary for gaining the sensitivity to adequately respond to the needs of the natural world and to the cultural needs of humanity. From the view of aesthetic perception, this should be the purpose of both art therapy and art education.

Sometimes I am asked for techniques, for example how to draw a hand. I say, "But there is no such thing as 'a hand.' Which hand do

---

[13] *Ibid.*

you want to draw? What is it doing? What is its intention? How is it feeling? What does it want to say? What is the image?" When a person focuses on the particularity of the unique image, the precise hand will appear in its singularity and clarity. No standard or conventional formula will do. One's thinking will be transformed from analytic to aesthetic. Of course the image does not have to be a picture on paper, it may be an idea or a feeling. As Jung said, these images are not replicas but intimations: the task is to give them body in this world— in our case by means of art materials. A person with a clear apprehension of the image no longer has to ask how to draw "a hand" because the hand is seen differently. "...there is a night time of the senses, and knowledge comes finally through a sixth sense, very much like the penetration of love."[14] Or, put more concisely by the poet Theodore Roethke, "In a dark time the eye begins to see."[15]

Aesthetic perception is a psychological experience not an activity of intellectual calculation. To begin to move aesthetic perception toward psychology, one must denounce the language of academic communications techniques and mass education to allow a psychology based in the work of Henry Corbin, Martin Heidegger, James Hillman, C. G. Jung, and Russell Lockhart, among others, to emerge. This "new psychological spirit" first proposed by Hillman in *The Myth of Analysis*[16] is based on an imaginal consciousness and a symbolic life style where the imaginal process is a form of aesthetic perception.

Hillman's approach is nonlinear and is guided by the psyche acting on the present, past, and future simultaneously. With its indirect access to the light (consciousness) and the dark (the numinous), the psyche works circularly and repetitiously. Unwilling to present straight answers which are measurable and provable, the psyche often does not function the way the ego would like it to. (Hillman insists that the ego of will and reason, recognizing itself by development, feels caught, compelled, or even guilty in the circularity of the psyche.) As will and reason conceive adaptation in terms of controlling and understanding reality, the psyche conceives in terms of the reality of the image.

[14] Gilbert Durand, "Psyche's View," *Spring 1981* (Dallas: Spring Publications, 1981), 14.

[15] Theodore Roethke, *The Collected Poems* (Garden City, New Jersey: Doubleday, 1966), 239.

[16] James Hillman, *The Myth of Analysis* (Evanston, Ill.: Northwestern UP, 1972).

The circular reconnaissance of the psyche can be seen in the process of epistrophe—leading a thing or event back to its archetypal roots. This process is echoed in aesthetic perception, where extension in space and time is both backward and forward as well as downward and inward. Again Schaefer-Simmern provides the best example of someone who practiced such circularity in his therapy and teaching.

Schaefer-Simmern encouraged his students to look carefully again and again at their drawing to see if they could improve upon it, each time getting closer to getting it just right. This technique has been criticized by art educators and art therapists who want to see quick progress and growth. While they may urge the patient or student to abandon these seemingly sterile reiterations, aesthetic perception requires such circularity. When one considers the past as part of the future and the present, "past" no longer means events gone by, completed or closed. Instead the past becomes the living roots of present and future, roots from which present imperatives receive their sustenance. Schaefer-Simmern seemed to understand that it is through circular reiteration that the image gains richness and body in the conscious world and finally achieves its essential form. This is how image feeds psyche.

John Constable is an artist who allowed image to feed psyche and who painted the things that he loved from his childhood. "The sound of water escaping from mill dams, willows, and old rotten planks, slimy posts and brickwork; I love such things," he said. "I shall never cease to paint such places."[17] His father was a miller and these childhood pleasures never left Constable: they were the very reiteration of his soul's imperative. While Constable is less concerned with representing the reality of water and mill ponds than he is with realizing their significance in his life, it would be a mistake to attempt to translate the *archai* or archetypes he paints as a way to understand Constable's life. Such discussion would lose those very images of mill dams, willows, old rotten planks, slimy posts. And what rich images they are! They open one's imagination in innumerable directions: stories of millers; the power of flowing water; water over the dam; leaking vessels; the underworld of slime and decomposition; willows bending in the wind; dams and blocked flow of water; mills and the

---

[17] John Constable, *Life and Letters of John Constable* (London: Chapman and Hall, 1896), 104-05.

grain of life. It is these images which are the *archai*, the primordial images which take us beyond Constable's own literal life and into a more universal realm. According to Jung these images are more than personal:

> The primordial images are the most ancient and the most universal "thought forms" of humanity. They are as much feelings as thought; indeed they lead their own independent life rather in the manner of part-souls as can easily be seen in those philosophical or Gnostic systems which rely on perception of the unconscious as the source of knowledge. The idea of angels or archangels, principalities and powers in St. Paul, the archons of the Gnostics, the heavenly hierarchy of Dionysus the Areapogate, all come from the perception of the relative autonomy of the archetypes.[18]

Thus for Jung images derive from the unconscious psyche and therefore are archetypal.

In her book, *Rosegarden and Labyrinth: A Study in Art Education*, Seonaid Robertson shows us the importance of such archetypal themes in art education.[19] Despite its aim toward educators, this book has been called by some the most important book in print for art therapists. Robertson tells us in the book that when such archetypal themes were elicited from high school students, something in the classroom changed.

> [The students demonstrated]...an exceptional degree of concentration while working; through a personal satisfaction in the results out of proportion to the actual achievement, as though these painters were actually seeing through the work to something beyond it; and through the effect of the finished work on myself and others, which acted like an incantation in poetry or the rhythms of Buddhist or Byzantine art, suggesting much more than it stated.[20]

---

[18] C. G. Jung, *Two Essays on Analytical Psychology* (Princeton: Princeton UP, 1966), § 104.

[19] Seonaid M. Robertson, *Rosegarden and Labyrinth, op. cit.*

[20] *Ibid.*, 81.

While Robertson suggests aesthetic perception deepens through circularity, Gilbert Durand gives the "new psychological spirit" the image of the uroborus, a mythical serpent devouring its own tail. Rather than an antithetical approach, this uroboric course is both metaleptic (guided by the aims of desire, present synchronicity and past causality) and metabolic (repetitive and differentiating). Rather than one track linear deduction, aesthetic thinking is more discontinuous and multivocal. This circulatory approach is metabolic in that it repeats the idea in many different images. It is metalyptic because it introduces the world by its past roots and is followed by new images and analogies. The emphasis here is on the "meta" (meaning between, behind, beyond, transforming, and change) rather than on "anti" (meaning against, opposite). The results of aesthetic perception are shadowy hints and intimations, but they enrich and deepen our perception as we forego the bright light of reason and the certainty of proof.

In Psyche's myth she is forbidden to see her beautiful husband, Eros, and at the end she is forbidden to see the beauty sent by Persephone, Queen of the Dead. Thus this myth tells us that Eros and Thanatos are not opposites, as Freud would have it, but Eros is a facet of Thanatos: Eros contains Thanatos (that inhibiting component that holds back life). With his torch upside down, Eros is also a symbol of death. Thanatos "leads life into the invisible psychic realm, 'below' and 'beyond' mere life, endowing it with the meanings of the soul given by death."[21] To illuminate intuition (the intimations of psyche), the simple view is inadequate. Learning how to draw a hand will not suffice because it lacks the spark of Eros. It is a mere generalization. No "how to draw it" formulas can be adequate. Proper adaptation would require cherishing the specific image—its uniqueness—which alone gives body to the essential reality. Reproducing the anatomy of a person without expressing strength or weakness, brutal moods or tenderness, would be, by comparison, merely tedious.

Art therapy and art education should be concerned with the deeper world, "below" and "beyond" generalization for they seek the realm of psyche's images. For centuries artists and poets have been aware that their work can give form to this reality. Michaelangelo articulated it well in poetry when he wrote, "[H]eaven-born, the soul a

---

[21] James Hillman, *The Myth of Analysis, op cit.*, 77.

heavenward course must hold / Beyond the visible world she soars to seek, / For what delights the eyes is false and weak / Ideal form, the universal mold."[22]

Although Michaelangelo's words are insightful, it may be helpful to turn once again to Schaefer-Simmern for a more recent example. In *The Unfolding of Artistic Activity*, Schaefer-Simmern throws light on autonomous mental processes which have been too little recognized.

> It is through these processes that man is able to comprehend sensuously the appearance of the world and to express his comprehension symbolically by means of the artistic form…The origin of artistic production can therefore only be found in the spiritual being of man himself, specifically in a definite sensation and a precise feeling for form that is constantly governed by visual conceiving, which in turn is spontaneously realized by a self sustained visual organization of form. Consequently it seems impossible to attain artistic form by advising students to compose a pictorial work according to special rules of outwardly predetermined pictorial effects.[23]

Artistic activity is seen by Schaefer-Simmern as an autonomous operation, independent of abstract thinking and based on sensuous creation and visual conception. Efforts of composition by academic principles of design, color harmony, and rules of perspective merely conceptualize the creative process and lead the artist away from a "definite sensation and a precise feeling for form." Schaefer-Simmern is not talking about visual perception but about visual conception; a kind of conception or knowledge that is independent of conceptual intellectual calculation, and which originates in a person's spiritual being. This is related to aesthetic perception. It can be seen as the intermediate realm of the psyche, a realm of ideal images or archetypal figures, of subtle substance and immaterial matter.

[22] Michaelangelo, from "Non vider gli occhi miei cosa mortale" *Michaelangelo: A Self Portrait*, Robert J. Clements, ed.(Englewood Cliffs, New Jersey: Prentice-Hall, 1963), 83. Editor's note: This stanza in Italian reads, *e se creata a Dio non fusse equale, / altro che 'l bel di fuor, c'agli occhi piace, / più non vorria; ma perch'è sì fallace, / trascende nella forma universale.*

[23] Henry Schaefer-Simmern, *The Unfolding of Artistic Activity* (Berkeley: The University of California Press, 1948), 188-89.

It is helpful to turn to poetry to illustrate what is meant here by archetypal figures. William Blake wrote that the source of poetic creation springs from archetypal elements:

> Poetic genius is the true man, and that the body or out-
> ward form of man is derived from the poetic genius.
> Likewise that the forms of all things are derived from their
> Genius, which by the ancients was called an Angel and
> spirit and demon.[24]

Like Blake, when I speak of angels, myths, and the gods, I take these to be *daimones*, not literal creatures to be worshipped in dogmatic sects or to be tested by scientific methods.

Blake was not alone in recognizing that poetry originates with something more than the personal. Percy Bysshe Shelly also said that poetry is created not by the poet but by "that imperial faculty whose throne is curtained within the invisible nature of man."[25] And, he adds, a poem is the very image of life expressed in its eternal truth and it is something divine. Another poet, Ranier Maria Rilke, found the angel a particularly important metaphor in portraying the proper reverence for the image as a message from the below and beyond. "This world, regarded no longer from the human point of view, but as it is within the angel, is perhaps my real task..."[26] For Rilke this invisible world holds a value often not appreciated. "The angel of the *Elegies* is the being who vouches for the recognition of a higher de-gree of reality in the invisible—therefore terrible to us because we, its lovers and transformers, still depend on the visible."[27]

The recognition of this invisible essence is necessary for aes-thetic perception. Beginning with shapes, aesthetic perception is not dependent on fact and reason, yet it knows what shape things are in. It unfolds for those who can allow being to be. Painter Max Beckman explained how this process influenced how he approached the canvas:

---

[24] William Blake, *Blake: Complete Writings*, Geoffrey Keynes, ed. (Oxford: Oxford UP, 1972), 98.

[25] Percy Bysshe Shelley, "A Defense of Poetry," *English Romantic Writers*, David Perkins, ed. (New York: Harcourt Brace Janovich, 1967), 1074.

[26] Maria Rainer Rilke, *The Duino Elegies*, J. B. Leishman and Stephen Spender trans., (New York: W. W. Norton, 1936), 88.

[27] *Ibid.*, 87.

> What I want to show in my work is the idea which hides
> itself behind so-called visible reality. I am seeking the
> bridge which leads from the visible to the invisible, like
> the famous cabalist once said, if you want to get hold of
> the invisible, you must penetrate as deeply as possible into
> the visible.[28]

This invisible, imaginal reality can be neither proven nor disproved
by means of ordinary argumentation. Modern physicists have concluded that matter in its deepest reality is mysterious because it is not
visible, not because we do not yet have instruments powerful enough,
but because it is by nature invisible. Gary Zukav, in his book *The
Dancing Wu Li Masters: An Overview of the New Physics*, writes that mysticism, psychology, and physics meet in language:

> Mystics from both the East and the West who claim to
> have beheld "the face of God" speak in terms so similar
> to [the language of particle physics] that any psychologist
> who professes an interest in altered states of awareness
> scarcely can ignore this obvious bridge between the disci-
> plines of physics and psychology.[29]

The realm of aesthetic perception is external to the ego, but it is
not in the physical world. It is neither subjective nor objective but
rather receptive, coming from the psyche. The logic of aesthetic perception is neither one of identity nor one of antithesis, neither realistic
representation nor intellectual abstraction. It is seeing into the psychic reality of things. Its goal in therapy is not so much to alleviate
burdens, to solve problems, or to keep the ego healthy and happy as
it is to ascertain the intention of the objective psyche. If we speak of
centering, we would mean putting the psyche at the center. Since the
ego and the psyche are not the same, to put psyche at the center
would inevitably mean to displace ego from that position. Therefore
this kind of centering would feel like imbalance to the ego and must
be distressing. The psyche is the place of origin for those necessary
symbolic realities which cannot be directly known by the ego. Thus

---

[28] Max Beckman, "On My Painting," *Modern Artists on Art*, Robert L. Herbert,
ed. (Englewood Cliffs, New Jersey: Prentice Hall, 1964), 132.
[29] Gary Zukav, *The Dancing Wu Li Masters: An Overview of the New Physics* (New
York: Bantam Books, 1979), 197.

the responsibility of the ego becomes that of stepping aside, off center, to allow psyche to speak. It means having enough respect for the image that we act on those hints and intimations without manipulating the message.

Aesthetic perception demands participation in imaginal reality and the embodiment of psychic image in daily encounters. An art experience can be a first step in realizing the beauty of our daily lives. It is not enough to write down one's dreams or to paint inner images, one must also connect such images to daily life. Connecting psychic image to daily life is the essence of creativity. Psychic participation has since ancient times been unconscious. Yet if we do not develop conscious participation, technological creativity may destroy the earth. Unless we develop conscious participation with psyche, humankind is in grave danger. The issue is not a scientific one. In the deepest sense it is a moral issue. "It is a question of initiation and ritual," Lockhart said. "It is a way of life, having more to do with religion and artistic traditions than with science."[30]

It was once common for initiation ritual to begin with an experience designed to eliminate the initiate's conscious ego concerns in order to help forget our common literal view.[31] The initiate was then taught how to remember—not the past, but the future, what one would experience at the heart of the ceremony, the spontaneous numinous events one would encounter in the depths of the temple—thus becoming a *therapeutes*. For our purposes here the second step in our initiation into a new psychological spirit will be to remember and accept the psyche as an autonomous reality. This psyche is not only personal but collective. Imagination is a function as real as the physical function of sight. Images—real but invisible forms—are the subject matter of art which gives them body. They can be the source of learning and of healing. In this process we must forget ego concerns such as, "I can't draw a straight line," "It doesn't look like a real cow," "What does my dream mean," "How will art therapy help me to get well, or to get a better job?" Here we are looking for the spontaneous spark of the psyche which has been obfuscated not only by subjectivism and the ego, but also by inattention and lack of devotion to psyche's images.

---

[30] Lockhart, *op. cit.*
[31] *Ibid.*

The Five Principles

Art education and art therapy begin to open us to the eternal worlds of everyday things once the collective unconscious is recognized. In this view the goal of art therapy is not to cure patients of their discomforts or to operate on the patient's problem in order to remove the patient's unacceptable behavior. Such attitudes leave little room for consideration of the patient's psyche. Instead the goal is to tap the creative potential which lies in the imagination through getting in touch with the ordinary.

This shift can be difficult, even painful, for those who have been trained in traditional art techniques. Students sometimes feel angry or confused when asked to disregard what they have been taught by previous art teachers—design principles, color harmony, proportion, perspective, and so on. The learning and competent use of such principles and rules is what had made them stand out as superior or talented art students. I remember when I first understood the shock this shift can cause. A capable young student who had received the highest grades in all her classes broke into tears in my class and cried, "You have taken away all the basic principles of art and left us with nothing to stand on." Although I thought I had given the students something to stand on—their response to reality and imagination, their curiosity about life and the interrelations of shapes—I realized then that a teacher has a responsibility to support students when they are required to disregard conventional techniques.

Many art educators claim that learning the traditional rules and principles of art is necessary in order to tame and discipline the immature and crude expression of enthusiastic, emotional students. In this view students must first learn how to make a tree look like a tree and a person look like a person. However if we would spend as much effort and time teaching students to express their responses to ordinary things as we now spend teaching the rules of proportion and perspective, students would achieve more genuine artistic results and would therefore be creating a healthier world. This aspect of art is not only therapeutic but is the basic element in all learning. An art experience is as close as anything in our world today to the direct experiencing of the creative imagination which shapes us and the world in which we live.

The following five basic principles help achieve this art experience: 1) give form; 2) work for clarity; 3) care enough; 4) never generalize; and 5) stick to the image. This last principle is intended to suggest the divine radiance in ordinary things. It is based on the Chinese artist-teacher who once told his students, "If you wish to draw a tree, look first to see if it is inside you." Wordsworth, in his poem "Imitations of Immortality," puts it another way:

> The earth and every common sight,
> To me did seem
> Apparelled in celestial light,
> The glory and the freshness of a dream.

One can deliteralize these five basic principles by seeing them not as a system, not as principles or rules, but as a method of imaginal perception; a way of being open to the mythical and metaphorical grids which rule our lives.

II

Give Form

The cosmos of things, their arrangement, displays archetypal
patterns; the world's soul is subject to depth psychological
analysis because imagination takes place in the construction of things as much as it takes place in the order of words.
—*James Hillman*

Art can be defined as an arrangement or pattern of shapes and
ideas which give form to the images that reside in the cosmos of objects. Contrary to what many believe, the world of
objects is not a world of dead matter. Objects, too, ask for recognition and respect. Scientific analysis and measurement has been the
sole criteria for "proof," but the actual effects of imaginal thinking
constitute a greater power in our lives. Psyche is not only human:
there is soul in matter. A psychological reality can be recognized as
the soul of an object, and this psychological content can be made
concrete through art-making. The only way to cope with skepticism
is to pay attention to the objects themselves, to see the minutia in the
pattern, shape, or form of the object. It requires imagination to see
that these details are the way that the object presents itself.

It is helpful here to turn to mythology from early Western culture. Gods and goddesses serve as archetypal paradigms of the way
human beings and material things present themselves during daily
encounters. This is not to take gods and goddesses literally as holy
figures to be worshipped. The gods are the articulation of that background in the collective psyche in which the great decisions of historical

importance take place, decisions which frame the life and thought of
each historical period. Thus we can establish and cultivate a psychological connection to the past which would not be possible without
these images.

Many attempts to use mythology remain in the domain of conceptual cognition, never reaching an imaginal or psychological mode
of thinking. Some "New Age" thinkers turn to spiritual ideas, leaving
both matter and soul out of the picture. The "subtle body of the
image" is not a literal thing. Metaphorical insight does not require a
para-world, a literal heaven somewhere up in the sky, separate from
the physical world. Rather, metaphorical seeing is a vision within the
psychological act of aesthetic perception. Imagination (metaphorical
seeing) is an operation that works in this world, the world of our
daily senses. It has no other place of operation. Only a soulless psychology would speak of sense data apart from the image in which the
data is presented.

Although popular terms such as "imagery" and "visualization"
seem to offer new kinds of content, these ideas are usually presented
in the same literal and linear mode aimed at willful control and pragmatic ends. As much as I want to avoid a literal, pragmatic bias, I
want equally to avoid a spiritual mysticism of auras, channeling, and
"twice-born man." Such mystical expressions move us away from an
archetypal psychology and into metaphysics. For our purposes here,
imagination must remain in the world of the senses. But what is sensed
must be perceived metaphorically and poetically.

Metaphorical Thinking

Poetry gives us metaphors to help us better understand this connection to the divine without falling into spiritualism. For Blake,
the imagination is the bosom of God, and human response expands
the bosom of God. This image-making power of the autonomous
psyche is not the work of human will and reason: it is numinous. In
his poem "Auguries of Innocence," Blake asks his reader to pay attention to the details of—and the gods within—the objects:

> To see the world in a Grain of Sand
> And Heaven in a Wild Flower

> Hold Infinity in the palm of your hand
> and Eternity in an Hour.[1]

In our secular age we have become unconscious of these psychic images. Even the ordinary things and events of our daily lives are permeated by the uninvited images which the world psyche presents in everything that surrounds us.

The title of Blake's poem "Auguries of Innocence," invokes the *Augures*, early Roman priests who observed the heavens, the flight of birds, visions and dreams, as well other unusual occurrences. It was the duty of these priests to inform the authorities whether the gods approved of their plans for the future. However the *Augures* could do little more than advise, and they lacked the power to make changes in the secular world. For Blake, the secular day-world which is cut off from the world of the *Augures* is not seeing the truth.

> We are led to Believe a Lie
> When we see With, not thro' the Eye
> Which was Born in a Night to perish in a night
> When the Soul Slept in Beams of Light.
> God Appears and God is Light
> To those poor Souls who dwell in Night.
> But does a Human Form Display
> To those who dwell in Realms of day.[2]

This poetic way of seeing can be applied to art education and art therapy. If we ask how to draw, we are assuming that there is an authority who knows the "right way." We are turning to the secular for explanation, interpretation, orthodoxy, and tradition. In Blake's language, it is for those who dwell in the night of "not Knowing" that the will of the gods is made clear. Only when we dwell in the twilight realms of the unconscious psyche can we realize—or make real—through art in our case—the value of ordinary things. Only in this realm can we imagine the archetypal roots of our individual experiences. Only in humility and acceptance of the autonomy of the objective psyche can the image be formed with concrete materials. This is where art begins. This is why the spontaneous drawings of

---

[1] William Blake, *Blake: Complete Writings*, Geoffrey Keynes, ed. (Oxford: Oxford UP, 1972), 433-4.

[2] *Ibid.*

children, untutored adults, and art therapy clients may be called art. They are formed psychic expression of the inner seer.

Even today, nearly two centuries after Blake's poem, many of us remain unaware of the role of imagination in our daily tasks. We deny the autonomous image-making proclivity of the psyche. Many do not see that the ordinary things and events of our daily lives are permeated by the uninvited images psyche presents and that ordinary daily objects display their soul in their sensuous forms. Our present way of seeing was shaped by secular images and assumptions about reality. The value of art education and art therapy is that it can "open the eternal worlds" and even expand "the bosom of God." In other words, it can expand the imagination.

Imagination is not simply a faculty of each individual. It is part of the "collective conscious." While the collective *un*conscious described by Jung has been explored in countless writings, the idea of a collective conscious—the beliefs, attitudes, behaviors, and emotions of a culture which are held in common—is still uncharted. This collective conscious is being formed by each individual's participation in the culture. Art is one activity where imagination can become something other than "mine." Where Barfield used the word "participation" to describe the processes by which we bring the invisible reality (the image) into visible form, one could also use the word "imagination.

Often painters and sculptors say they feel a thing come into existence as though it had a life of its own, as though it could speak its way into being through the hands of the artist. In this way artists have an inner vision of the "true ideas" of ordinary things and participate in reality. It is this kind of participation which is therapeutic. Thus a reverence for the image is the goal of both art therapy and art education.

Giving form to the invisible image is the work of art-making. However this form is not a simple representation of nature. Rather it is a presentation of the image. It is giving form to something that has (although it is invisible) a very real existence. A psychological image has no physical existence whatever. Yet it is a reality.

The Unconscious Psyche

The origin of conscious knowledge—cognition—is in the unconscious. This is an idea with a rich history. Plato portrayed all cognition as remembrance, as a "finding within," and St. Augustine knew that the mind has access to a storehouse of imaginal memory over and against the light of consciousness. In human beings life manifests itself as psyche, the first level of which is the unconscious, connecting us with all life, both as nature and as spiritual principle, which inheres in and transcends nature—*anima mundi*. C. G. Carus (1789-1869) maintained an ideal vision without leaving the actualities of the psyche and its unconscious. He conceived mankind's link to nature to be through the unconscious psyche. The psychic force, he says, "absolutely dominates and pervades matter, it creates while still completely absorbed in itself as if dreaming or thinking in shapes, because it can not yet think in concepts."[3]

Here, then, is the basis for the first principle, "giving form." Art comes from the unconscious psyche and is prior to conscious cognition, creating as if dreaming or thinking in shapes, because it cannot yet think in concepts. Once again, Hillman gives art therapists and educators a psychological language to flesh out this idea:

> …the only way we can get at the soul of the object is to think of it as a form or as a shape or a face, an image, and it displays its own image, its imagination. So it has subjectivity.[4]

"Giving form" means seeing the object as the face of an image and providing concrete shape to the invisible image. The object becomes animated—we see it as a face—and it displays its own image.

> The object is a phenomenological presentation with its own depth and complexity, in a context of relationships in the world. It has a history and so, a memory, with its own subjectivity. Art-making is an aesthetic appreciation of how things present themselves in a particular shape, indicating what shape they are in. Things are ensouled and speak to the imagination.[5]

---

[3] C. G. Carus, *Psyche* (New York: Spring Publications, 1970), 29.
[4] James Hillman, *Inter Views* (Dallas: Spring Publications, 1983), 132.
[5] *Ibid.*

Following this idea, it is not the object the artist draws or paints. Instead the object tells us what shape it is in, its face, its image, and we give it form. Thus the image is made visible in the form. Forms in themselves have no value. If seen only in their outer shape they are empty idols. It is what they are committed to express: it is their soul that gives objects a face. Thinking of the thing as a form requires thinking of form differently. We must think of form as an active force.

This leads to an important corollary to the first principle: think of form as an active force speaking to imagination. An object or shape may be sitting or hanging, it may be standing or lying, or it may be moving. Even in a painting we imagine movement from object to object. Some shapes "move" while others seem immobile. But it is not enough to see objects in this general way. Art, if it is anything, is careful and precise expression. Shapes may sit solidly, precariously, tentatively, or restfully. And the particular way they do this ordinary thing—sitting—manifests a precise expression. Movement may be smooth, staccato, or rhythmic. It may be quick, gay, ponderous, sly, or direct. Or an object may rise, climb, or float, spring or soar. It may fall—tumbling, drifting, plummeting. To "think of form as an active force" one must ask "What's happening?" The shape of a thing may be sharp and cutting, puncturing, slicing, piercing, pricking, hacking, or sawing. Or it may be soft or dull. A shape may scream for attention, or it may be shy and retiring. It may be angry or soothing, rejecting or protecting. Forms may dance or march or trudge or trot. And the dance could be a waltz or a polka, a cancan or a jig.

It is essential for art therapists to think of form as an active force, as an image doing something. A painting speaks but it speaks in images through form. It is communication. But true communication cannot be a contrived attempt to convey an already formed idea. It must be a result rather than a goal. If one already knows what will be communicated, then it is more like propaganda than true communication.

Two still-lifes by Chardin may be helpful examples. Both paintings are kitchen still-lifes yet their color and mood are quite different. One, in the Ashmolean Museum at Oxford, (**fig. 3**) is more lively and dynamic. The colors are brighter and the objects fill the pictorial field more completely. In the other, a still-life now held at the Museum of Fine Art, Boston (**fig. 4**) the objects sit on the table in a dark room

almost as though they were stored on a shelf in a closet. Even the
table in the Oxford picture is more dynamic in shape with a curved
edge and a sharp corner protruding near the viewer. There are fewer
objects of food here but they are larger and more vital . The fish,
though cut open to display the blood-red wound, is lying in an arch
similar to the natural curve of a fish flipping to get back into the
water. The two eggs near the edge seem ready to roll off at the
slightest jolt of the table. The large pot is open and is tilted against
the wall with its gapping mouth toward the viewer and the large
black pitcher is echoed in dark brown on the opposite side of the
painting. The container's roundness, rather than its verticality, is emphasized. In the Boston painting the large pot is sitting solidly on the
table and it is covered with a lid. The verticality of the white pitcher
is emphasized by the vertical movement of the two ends of the
white cloth hanging from the edge of the table. The total effect is of
a group of objects sitting solidly on a shelf.

We give body to the image by means of enumerating the parts—
accounting or recounting the story. This is a recital that brings the
invisible images into the world of the senses and differentiates them.
Thus the image becomes more precise. Such a recital is one means of
making differentiation visible. Precise description gives an account
of what is happening. It can be an imaginal ritual with great force,
giving body to the psychological image, seeing things as vital form.
Their arrangement, their attitudes, the interrelations of their parts display archetypal patterns. Imagination takes place in giving form, seeing
the true face of things.

A common—and dangerous—misconception is that design is the
end result of art. Distortion, "disproportion," and the absence of
linear perspective are accepted only if the resulting work achieves a
"pleasing" design in "harmonious" colors. Harmony—the pleasing
arrangement of lines, colors and shapes—is taken to be the goal of
composition. This is a half-truth, and it obscures the more authentic
purpose of design to reveal the invisible through the visible.

It is true that order is important in art, but only as a means of
creating that specific form which will express the artist's unique image and his or her relation to it, not for the sake of harmony or for

the sake of leading a patient away from disorder toward a happier frame of mind. The subject matter in a work is an essential part of its total expression, but the therapeutic and educational value of art is obtained only when the structure is given equal consideration with the subject matter. Art reveals, through visual means, an awareness of the human situation. The artist's purpose must remain singular— to discover his or her unique relationship to the world and to the reality of the psychological sphere which is autonomous and collective as well as personal.

Art carries the image of the artist's psychic state through both the subject matter and the way it is depicted. There is no such thing as an objective view of a fixed reality. When Cezanne, the father of modern art, said that he wanted to realize—"bring into being"—his visual apprehension of nature, he was speaking of giving form to his individual response to reality. At the same time he was proclaiming the new world-view that man, by the process of perception, becomes a part of the object perceived, and by creative imagination the object comes into being through the participation of man, in that unknown something that religions through the ages have called gods. Reality does not consist of the thing-in-itself, absolute and isolated. Reality is the encounter of human consciousness with the thing perceived. The reality of objects can only be known through the personal experience of them, which in turn colors and becomes part of that reality. Artistic form is the realization of this force in the things of ordinary experience. It is not mere representation. Form comes from psychic energy.

Cezanne's revolutionary attitude toward art as form-giving, recognizes the fact that in order to bring one's apprehension of reality into being it is necessary to mold or adjust the material perceived in such a way as to retain in the work of art the vital intensity found in nature. Cezanne wanted to give the painting a form which has vitality and tension equal to, though not the same as, that created in his intense encounter with nature. Form expresses both nature and the painter's experience.

Giving form as artistic expression is a concept already put to use in poetry, psychology, and philosophy. Poet Charles Olson described a poem as "energy transferred from where the poet got it, by way of the poem itself, all the way over to the reader."[6] Gestalt psychologists, particularly Rudolf Arnheim, give us an aesthetic theory of art based especially on form—form as a total gestalt and as the expressive element *par excellence*. Arnheim's delineation of the hidden structure of the pictorial field can be of genuine value in helping a teacher or therapist to avoid mere projection or personal preferences in the process of interpretation or evaluation.

Meaning and Structure

Unfortunately some art therapists feel that no interpretation of art work can be made, that any aesthetic interpretation is irrelevant, and that psychological interpretation must be based solely on what the patient says about the work (i.e. "The patient who made the work is the only one who knows what it means"). If this were so, art therapy would amount to no more than a mental exercise and a therapist would be superfluous. The process of artistic formation is where the healing takes place, yet this process remains mysterious to the artist as well as to the teacher or therapist. The therapist or teacher encourages the patient or student to develop a relationship with the art work, for that is where growth and healing take place. But to do this the therapist or teacher must know something about how to read the image as it is displayed in the artistic structure. It is the quality of aesthetic formation in the art work which is educational and therapeutic, and it is the development of this quality which the art teacher or art therapist must learn to read. The artistic structure provides a clue to the psychological state of the artist. What speaks is not only the subject matter but the surface pattern. Form in art is always created in a total context, but it is structure that tells us most about the meaning. First we begin by just looking at the image—experiencing it, respecting what is there. Sometimes this is enough. Sometimes the image is so clearly stated that no further elaboration is necessary. However, as a rule, more is required before we understand what the work is saying.

---

[6] Charles Olson, "Projective Verse," *Charles Olson: Selected Writings*, Robert Creeley, ed. (New York: New Directions, 1951), 16.

Let us consider Edvard Munch's well-known lithograph "The Scream" (**fig. 5**) as an example of finding meaning in structure. First we feel fear and instability. It is the structure rather than the subject—a person with open mouth—that tells us things are on the verge of collapse. There is a pulsating echo reverberating throughout the form. We can say this, not because of the content but because of the structure. In the center foreground there is a screaming figure with its hands holding its head and covering its ears. The lower part of its body or legs is cut off by the bottom edge of the picture. The figure is on a bridge which spans a deep chasm on the right. Behind the figure and to the left, are two other figures walking on the bridge, very stable and upright. In the distance, behind the central figure, is a lake with two boats and at the end of the lake to the right of center is a barely suggested village with a church steeple. The sky is cloud streaked in undulating waves while the bridge railing runs in deep perspective from the lower right-hand corner of the picture past the central figure to the figures on the left.

We can say that the mood is one of fear and instability, not just because of the facial features but also because of the formal structure. The foreground figure is pushed into the lower half of the pictorial field, with head "pinned" to the exact center but hanging to the right below center. Weak wrists and hands covering the ears add to the dangling, wavering quality of head and body, which sways, legless in an arc. The form of a chasm is created between the screaming figure and the figures receding to the left. The swift perspective of the bridge and the length of the railing separating the screamer and the other figures create a psychological chasm of separateness. The distant figures form a rectangle blocking the end of the bridge. There is no escape, the bridge has no beginning and no end.

The continuation of the diagonal curve constituting the edge of the earthly chasm would seem to sweep up the distant figures, the ships and village—perhaps all civilization—into the upper portion of the picture. Other curves constitute a swirling echo of the ovals of the mouth and head. Thus not only the subject matter but, more importantly, the quality of aesthetic formation connects one with the image and creates this mood.

Taking a closer look at the pictoral field gives us a more profound insight into the psychology of the painting (**fig. 6**). While the
screamer seems to dangle from the center point there is a split right
at the head which would blow the top off, so to speak. Formally the
figure is isolated and separated from the upper "populated" half of
the pictorial field. Not only is the foreground figure squeezed into
the central one fourth of the pictorial field, it is also enclosed in the
lower right-hand corner of the picture by an arc suggested by the
edge of the chasm and the left side of the swaying figure. The vertically oriented ovals of the mouth, head, and hands tie the figure
psychologically to the vertical drop of the chasm wall. The only other
strong vertical is that of the two figures which are attached to the left
edge of the frame. The rectangular shape suggested by these figures
is similar in proportion to that of the picture as a whole. The vertical
belongs to the screaming figure. The central vertical divides the figure, the head slightly to the right of this central axes and the body
slightly left of it. The lower body forms a circular movement that
leads over the railing. The formal element which counteracts the circular movement over the railing is the placement of the head which
is pinned precariously to the precise pictorial center. The tenuous
placement of the head in relation to the center point and just at the
juncture of the downward "V" shape which splits the lower portion
of the picture and the horizontal upper section with village, church,
and boats—and perhaps civilization.

The form emphasizes what the scene alone would suggest: that
the central figure is split, faltering, caught, and frightened. The split
is emphasized by the different focus of the two eyes, by the placement of the figure (half on each side of vertical center) and by the
opposing direction of movement of the upper and lower parts of
the body. The lower body, although placed left of center, suggests a
movement over the railing and into the chasm. The image is that of
being pulled both ways and blocked both ways—a feeling of stuckness.

The form also provides echoes and repetitions which give the
image its power. The screaming mouth is a vertically oriented oval
relating to the descending inverted pear-shaped, skull-like head, but
the echoing oval shapes suggested by the lake and undulating cloud
shapes are horizontally oriented. Cloud, steeple, hand and body form

a suggested question mark. The strong vertical lines of the chasm contrast sharply with the horizontal lines that circle the lake and the diagonal lines that form the railing. The movement which captures the eye is in the lower half of the painting, and the human figures are caught in the triangle formed by the railing.

If this were an art therapy client's drawing, one analogy after another probably would have struck home in regard to fantasies, behaviors, ambitions, attitudes toward self, life, sexuality, fears, abandonment, or stuckness. The image becomes more profound and gathers value as this pattern is recited and elaborated—"As the image takes shape the meaning becomes clear." Art is therapeutic simply because of this fact. However healing depends on developing a relationship to the image, making the pictorial meaning conscious, seeing the image reflected in one's everyday life, and establishing a dialogue with the image—a reciprocal relationship of friends, "befriending" the image. This renders words such as interpretation and hermeneutics—as it has come to be synonymous with interpretation—unnecessary. There is no scientifically objective or pure work with images. An image catches each of us in a complex and resonates, if it is to resonate at all, through the complex. That is why it is crucial always to derive our work from the image and always to return to the image.

Now let us apply our ideas to the drawing of an art therapy patient. (**fig. 7**) A man in his 50s, he was hospitalized because of unaccountable physical pains. His drawing depicts a memory of his childhood home and shows the contrast between a stable cattle ranch and a sheep ranch where, the patient said, "the sheep eat the grass faster than it can grow and if the shepherd didn't move them constantly they would eat the grass right into the ground and it would die." One could say that this picture shows a contrast between pleasant memories of unperturbed childhood and the current situation of unaccountable suffering and hospitalization. However it is more important to look at what inner psychological contrasts may exist (**fig. 8**).

A large house stands in the central lower portion of the drawing with a cowboy on his horse, a tree and a cow or steer are to the right, and a barn and windmill with water trough on the left. In the upper right portion of the picture a brown mountainous area is fenced off from the grassy prairie. A pale green form that is a cactus, three sheep, a shepherd, and shepherd's shack are also depicted on the mountain. The picture has a horizontal rectangular format, the proportion being approximately two thirds as high as wide. This stretches the image in the direction of the horizontal and reinforces the tranquil mood. The level of the back of the cow lies slightly below the central horizontal axis, the bottom line of the foliage of the tree almost horizontal lies just above this axis, the top of the barn (minus the roof gable) is also horizontally just above this axis. The same line of the house is slightly below this axis and lower still is the horizontal top of the addition on the house and the back of the horse.

These elements cause a strong horizontal movement through the central area of the picture from edge to edge. Lower still, and giving a stability to the whole, are the bottom of the barn and the house. Rising from these horizontals are several vertical lines. On the central vertical axis we notice the left side of the door to the house, the implied peak of the roof, and the peak of the central mountain where the sheep herder tends his flock. To the right, the tree and the man on the horse offer a vertical emphasis, while to the left the barn and the windmill are both vertical structures. The windmill connecting house and barn reaches up to the top of the pictorial field. All of these vertical movements give a sense of dignity and stability. Even the diagonal aspects are stabilized, especially by the central position of the house with its roof line implicating the two diagonal axes and pinned securely by the peak of the roof located at dead center. The water trough is also related to this center point. The diagonal axis from lower left to upper right passes through the central point of the barn door, the edge and peak of the roof of the house (implied), and the mountain at the upper left corner of the picture. The "V" shape encompassing the mountain compliments the inverted "V" shape of the house and the mountains themselves. The shape of the main house is square. All of this causes even the diagonals in this image to be less dynamic and more contained than would be the case if they were not so closely tied to the stabilizing verticals and horizontals. The darker, fenced-off mountain area is the most dynamically active part of the picture, with its heavy wavy lines outlining the peaks and legs moving in various directions from the bodies of the sheep: this shadow world has the greater animation.

In the foreground the radiating branches of the tree are contained in the dark, heavy foliage. The radiating blades of the windmill
are tied to the top edge of the picture and the peak formed by the
legs of the structure. These elements give the image a serene and
stabilized feeling. If one did not know that the patient were hospitalized for unaccountable physical pain, one might suppose the painting
was done by a stable, well-adjusted person. Knowing that the painting was done by a man suffering significant physical pain some art
therapists might be tempted to assume that this apparent serenity is a
psychological denial, and they might attempt to treat the patient with
a dose of "reality testing." One might try to face the patient with the
contrast of the pictorial image to the daily reality of his life in an
effort to overcome the denial. However the very strength with which
the stability is formed would indicate that such a course would end in
failure. How then could the therapist help the patient befriend what
seems to be an image of psychological denial?

Archetypal Art Therapy

An archetypal art therapist might restate the various aspects of
the image in first person—a kind of ritual chanting of the image:

> When my house is large and centered I ride home on my
> horse. When I am sitting on my horse my house is near
> and the trough is filled with water. When the mountains
> are fenced off, everything is serene below. When things
> are centered and pleasant, there is still a corner of tran-
> sience and turbulence. When the sheep are scattered, I
> come riding home.

Or, picking up on color, a therapist might say:

> When I am blue, I return home to the house and ranch.
> When the foliage on the tree is heavy and dark the water-
> ing trough is full and I ride home. When the sheepherder
> is black and fenced out, the house and barn are in the fore-
> ground.

Or, we might even "eternalize" the image:

> Every time I ride home the sheep and mountains are dark
> and turbulent. Whenever the watering trough is full, the

house seems central and large. Whenever things are cen-
tered there is still a dark turbulent corner.

As we chant what is happening in the picture as though it were a
round or fugue, a deeper significance begins to resonate, giving more
and more possibility for connections to appear. As the patient is encouraged to restate the various aspects of the image in this way, his
paintings may begin to take on a different structural format. This
dialogue between the patient and his images is the very essence of art
therapy. It is more important that the patient establish this dialogue
with his art work than it is for him to establish a dialogue with the
therapist. The therapist is a sympathetic facilitator, the third person
who keeps the patient and the art work in communion. It is through
the art work itself that healing comes. It may be helpful to the patient
to talk with the therapist, but a change in pictorial structure is a more
reliable indication that psychological movement is taking place.

Although "childish," this drawing achieves "formed expression."
It has inner consistency and unity of form and content. Its formal
and expressive qualities are more the work of the unconscious than
of the ego: the ego thought that it wanted to make a realistic representation of a horse and rider, a cow, and a windmill, but he achieved
much more than that.

It is not our function as art teacher or art therapist to help the
client gain the skill to achieve realistic representation. Rather we need
to respect the hand's "inability" to do what the ego wishes and its
unconscious ability to express a truth which the ego does not yet know.

One might look at a work like that of this client as a narrative
story: the cowboy coming home after a hard day's ride. In the beginning the patient chose to interpret it this way—a sort of naive
realism—and telling a story is often the approach patients first take.
The picture might also be seen as a story about the artist's emotions
and feelings: the happy, even smug, rancher returning home to his big
house and watered grass is in sharp contrast to the wretched lot of
the sheepherder. Or if the patient identifies with the sheepherder, he
may feel resentment toward the cowboy. A third way to look at this
image would be through the lens of thematic symbolism: home becomes the great nurturing mother. When we begin to organize the
image according to a symbolic theme, we organize the parts in a certain

way—into mother, nurturing, security, and so on. We build into the image a second story. This second story is an interpretation of the image which usually relates more precisely to the symbolic theme than to the image itself. To see the image imagistically is more difficult and complex. As an image none of these symbolic themes is thrown out. All parts of the image are left intact, and none is singled out.

The reason for such ritual chanting of the parts of the picture—for carefully defining its form—is to keep ideas rushing into and through the vortex. Then there is no need to interpret. Ideas will begin to occur to the patient and he will say, "That's right," or "That fits," or "It's like when I do or feel this or that." The problem is how to do art therapy without turning the image into a diagnostic symbolic theme. Doing so would have a destructive impact on the soul of the image. Instead we must become more sensitive in reading the image.

III

WORK FOR CLARITY

I am the angel of reality...
I am the necessary angel of earth,
Since in my sight you see the earth again.
Cleared of its stiff and stubborn man-locked set,
And in my hearing, you hear its tragic drone.

—*Wallace Stevens*

There is no necessary opposition between
clarity and imagination.

—*James Hillman*

The content of art derives from our daily experiences, and those experiences are more than physical or conceptual events. They have the numinous quality of an angel—the necessary angel— of Henry Corbin's celestial earth. Viewed in this way the content of art would be the earth and everyday reality, cleared of its skepticism, materialism, and literalism. This is Romanticism, a response to the threat of skepticism and the denial that objects outside ourselves— including other people—can be really known.

Thus Romanticism is a response to a crisis of knowledge. This response is a quest for a return to the ordinary, or perhaps a *re*-quest for the return of the ordinary.[1] Allowing skepticism into our lives invites tragedy, and poets and philosophers have not missed this point. "Thoreau calls this everyday condition quiet desperation, Emerson

[1] Stanley Cavell, "In Quest of the Ordinary: Texts of Recovery," *Romanticism and Contemporary Criticism*, Morris Eaves and Michael Fischer, eds. (Ithaca: Cornell UP, 1986), 183*ff.*

says silent melancholy, Coleridge and Wordsworth are apt to say despondency or dejection; Heidegger speaks of it as our bedimmed averageness, Wittgenstein as our bewitchment; Austin both as a drunken profundity and as a lack of seriousness.[2] Accordingly we are meant to be human and to stumble. We need this sense of the everyday, the ordinary, the near, the low, to become intimate with the world of things which exists before our beliefs and our doubts. This creates a paradox: by not knowing we get closer to the primordial pre-knowledge of archetypal reality.

This leads to the second basic principle: work for clarity. Clarity demands imaginative insight. The clarity we seek is a psychological clarity to which we can adapt as if it were a habitat, an extraordinarily ordinary abode. In order to gain this order of clarity, we must give up the belief that humans are separate from nature, that only human beings have soul, and that only humans can make decisions. We must, at the very least, admit, along with modern physicists, that we are a part of a much larger organism such as the earth or the universe. We share soul with the rest of existence, and we must see through the poetic eyes of this world soul. If poiesis-making can bring us back to the things of everyday experience, can breathe life into the ordinary, then art must be concerned with our ordinary experiences, and the content of art will be our everyday thoughts, beliefs, hopes, and emotions.

According to Harold Rosenberg the artist's trade goes back to the oracles and soothsayers of ancient civilizations whose wisdom was gleaned from the gods. The words of the oracles were the motivation for and verification of state decisions, although the omens they produced concerned the inexpressible and unknowable. Modern science would say that to know the unknowable is not to know at all. However, "Not knowing is an eros moment, and if we linger there psyche begins to speak spontaneously."[3] To listen to the psyche is to gain psychological clarity. We need to linger with eros in the state of not knowing. But this is not an easy task as Lockhart says,

> We have difficulty staying in a state of not knowing [of
> stumbling pathology]... Whenever we don't know, the great

---

[2] *Ibid.*, 187

[3] Russell Lockhart, *Psyche Speaks: A Jungian Approach to Self and World* (Wilmette, Ill.: Chiron Publications, 1987), 45.

unknown intrudes ever so slightly, and the great unknown
is death... That is the secret power of the symbol, that is, in
Jung's sense of symbol as, "something that still belongs to
the domain of the unknown, or something that is yet to be."[4]

The old world is dying and a new world is not yet formed. In
such a transition of culture, the ordinary becomes a quest. In today's
commercial and consumer based society, as Hillman puts it, we have
become "thing sick." Things want to see and to be seen, they want us
to notice what shape they are in. They want us to care. In a culture
ruled by positivism, technology, behaviorism, and other materialist
ideas, the thing in its ordinariness is difficult to acknowledge. According to Heidegger we must take a step back and learn to think
another way to reach things.

> Thinking in this way we are called by the thing as the thing.
> In the strict sense of the German word, *bedingt*, we are
> "be-thinged," the conditioned ones. We have left behind
> us the presumption of all unconditionedness.[5]

Art therapists and art educators need to maintain this grounding
in the things and experiences of everyday life and to foster it in their
charges. Marion Richardson, an art educator who acknowledges "the
loveliness and the wonders of the world before us" in her method, is
an excellent example of showing the clarity of the image in her work.
She asked her young pupils to shut their eyes while they listened to
her description of a familiar scene and to draw or paint the scene
only when the image was clear in their minds. "Everywhere I looked,
the scene fell into a picture," she said. After she discovered this teaching technique:

> The work had a new quality... It now had an inner quality.
> In a vague, dark way I began to see that this thing we had
> stumbled upon, as it were almost by chance, was art, not
> drawing; something as distinct and special as love itself;
> and as natural. I could free it, but I could not teach it.[6]

---

[4] *Ibid.*

[5] Martin Heidegger, "The Thing," *Poetry Language Thought*, Albert Hoffstader,
trans. (New York: Harper & Row, 1971), 181.

[6] Marion Richardson, *Art and the Child* (London: University of London Press,
1948), 13.

With this method, the children's work had clarity, "whereas before it had been little more than the reproduction of something photographed by the physical eye, it now had an original, inner quality."[7]

Clarity of image can bring before us an apprehension of the *archai,* or archetype, of what appears. Each image is significant and has multiple implications for archetypal resonance in our lives. Archetypal psychology pays close attention to these archetypes which are personified in myths as gods and goddesses. These archetypes constitute the extraordinary in the ordinary.

The life of an artist is a life of beholding with reverence and respect. And "the life of beholding is a life of thinking," according to Heidegger, "For *theoria* is pure relationship to the outward appearance belonging to whatever presences, to those appearances that, in their radiance, concern man in that they bring the presence of the gods to shine forth."[8] *Thea,* meaning "truth" and *Orao,* meaning respect and reverence, are the roots of *Theoria* and "it is as goddess that *Alethea*, the unconcealment from out of which and in which that which presences, presences, appears…" The goddess here would of course be Aphrodite.

Conventional perception takes the literal content of a work of art, for example, as its meaning and significance. But every work of art is the objectification of an image, a poetic intuition. It is the result of an imaginative insight which acknowledges the world through archetypal figures because psychic images are the *archai*, the background patterns of all human behavior. The objectification of the image must be contained in a suitable form. The work of art results from a sudden flash of imaginative insight—the spark of psyche—which echoes the world we know. This is the archetypal world of psychic reality.

This sudden insight must be embodied in a structure which is the result of imaginative attention. "When you pay attention to the world, the world pays attention back to you, but the vehicle that began the attention is not commensurate with the immensity that comes back."[9]

[7] *Ibid.*

[8] Martin Heidegger, "Science and Reflection," *The Question Concerning Technology and Other Essays* (New York: Harper & Row, 1977), 164.

[9] David Whyte, *Poetry and the Imagination*, (Langley, Wash.: Many Rivers Co. Audio tape, not dated).

The world paying attention back to you is a therapeutic and educative force because of the immensity of the soul.

The everyday world is alive without our bidding and we see it only darkly. To get in touch with what we cannot bid or command requires an initiation through ritual (something as simple as a beauty hunt, which Richardson also promoted). The therapist or teacher cannot do it, but we can create a time and a place for attending to the world, with real devotion, and a ritual for paying attention. This sense of "shadow seeing" is a first clue to the clarity we seek. To get in touch with psychological reality requires an initiation, a ritual rather than logical analysis. It is an eros moment of not knowing, of waiting, lingering long enough to hear Psyche speak. To assuage the great unknown requires the secret power of symbolic thinking. It requires ritual, a ritual both of forgetting and of remembering; forgetting our academic concepts and remembering the image from the soul, a kind of brooding.

Art as Ritual

Even beauty must be seen with a psychological eye, must be seen from the shadowy underworld of the soul. Ritual is perhaps the clearest way to reach a precise differentiation between an imaginal approach and a diagnostic- or data-based approach. Thomas Moore calls ritual a moving act of imagination. The word ritual means "to flow, run, rush or stream. A 'rite' is a river, *rivus*—river or stream... One arrives, or 'de'-rives by approaching or leading from the river."

> To be in ritual is to be in Joyce's river, flowing in a Viconian circle or cycle that includes Eve and Adam's place, the rivers of paradise and the Parents, and that continually flowing stream where they can say: Here comes everybody... To be in ritual is to be like Tristan, rudderless, without a steering ego, but equipped with a musical instrument, an imagining ego... To be in ritual is not simply to be adrift, but to be adrift with an instrument that is not a rudder. A ritual sense gives life to the ten thousand things, to multiplicity unimaginable.[10]

---

[10] Thomas Moore, *Rituals of the Imagination* (Dallas: Pegasus Foundation, 1983), 1.

There are two things worth noting in this excerpt: first the inclusion of everybody, Adam's abode, and the cycle of past, to present to future and back, and second, a steering ego being replaced by an imagining ego. An imaginal art-making is different from a cognitive- or discipline-based art education or diagnosis based on the standard diagnostic manual, the *Diagnostic and Statistical Manual* of the Analytical Psychiatric Association, also known as the DSM-4. It is important to maintain this differentiation. "Whenever the light and heat of scientific consciousness are turned upon a field, they produce sudden proliferation, splitting the object under study into ten thousand aspects"[11]

We must give up some of the most cherished prejudices which we have inherited from the seventeenth century, a century of rational science in search of final and universal truth. In imaginal art-making we are left without a guiding rudder, but we are allowed a musical instrument—the imagination. This is not to advocate a simple spontaneity and egotistical outpouring. Rather it is a new discipline, a discipline of the imagination. The old discipline-based art education is merely an example of the cognitive, analytical and historical approach espoused by academic art education. It is a cognitive, not an imaginative, discipline. Even the emphasis on stages of development and self identity is merely rational. It is impossible to respect the uniqueness of the individual when we see stages of development, classes, and types. Only when we focus on the uniqueness of each individual can we see them clearly. "Of those so close beside me which are you/ God bless the ground. I shall walk softly there," writes the poet, Theodore Roethke.[12] It takes an angel, a god's blessing.

Religious Images

Sometimes a particular topic has become so common that it has become a rudder, steering us into stereotype and repetition. Likewise, religious pictures can become trite and sentimental. One fifth grade teacher, a Nun in a catholic school, when faced with this problem,

---

[11] James Hillman, *op. cit*, 29. Note the continuing expansion in the successive editions of the DSM from a small pamphlet in the beginning to the huge tome of the fourth edition.

[12] Theodore Roethke, *The Collected Poems of Theodore Roethke* (Garden City, New Jersey: Doubleday, 1965), 108.

found a helpful solution in the children's interest in stories of cowboys and Indians or cops and robbers. She approached the topic of the crucifixion obliquely. She told her pupils a story of bad guys ganging up on a good guy, beating him, betraying him, and at last hanging him. In discussing this theme, one of her pupils mentioned the rope used to hang the good guy. Only then did the teacher reveal to them that the story happened over a thousand years ago, and that at that time they hanged people by nailing them to a cross. The pupils then realized the familiar story was about Jesus Christ, but their emotional interest was already stirred up and their sense of justice aroused. The result was a compelling expression hardly to be expected from fifth grade children.

Taking a closer look at these drawings reveals how art can emerge from those who may not have mastered conventional skills. The austere face and staring eyes under heavy brows of the impressive portrayal of God in **figure 9** has a similar expressive power to that of a head of Christ by Rouault (**fig. 10**). Neither is realistic, yet both are images with authentic soul. The pathos and empathy expressed in the bruised head and face in **figure 11** is amazing. The lines and color, the resigned, closed eyes and the tilted head work together to portray the suffering of having been beaten. The drawing expresses a profound sorrow for a world of sin, to a degree hardly to be expected from a child. It would be difficult to find another depiction of the sharp inner pain of the sacrificed Christ than that of **figure 12**. The unexpected but effective use of a yellow-green outline around the nose adds to the acrid sting of the fate of this savior. Note the resignation and the tears welling in the eyes, which suggests an inner despair and passion.

Some of the children's drawings have elements which echo well-known forms of art. The drawing labeled **figure 13** is a rather simple and primitive depiction, but its direct presentation is reminiscent of the New Mexico Santos painted by the early Mexican settlers (**fig. 14**). Many of the early churches were decorated by untutored peasants in the 16th and 17th centuries. Yet this child had never seen such santos. Even an immature talent can achieve evocative expression when the subject matter is meaningful and compelling. The bleeding Christ in **figure 15** bears a striking resemblance to the wood carving of the Penitent Christ, (**fig. 16**) in Colorado Springs. The quiet suffering and tormented ordeal of misunderstood martyrdom—told as a "good guy" being beaten and murdered—seems to echo the confusion and despair that so many children experience.

None of these children were considered especially gifted or particularly interested in art. Most of them concentrated on the head of Christ, although this was not suggested. They express a concern for the underdog, for betrayal, and for stoic martyrdom. But these are depicted without routine or sentimental affect. There is a moral imperative in therapy and education. Maybe the purpose of these professions is to relieve the world of its "stiff and stubborn man-locked set," and its "tragic drone."

Religious pictures often are conventional and sentimental and lack a deep involvement from the artist. Creating an image so well known with emotion and reverence is not easy. Raphael painted more than fifty pictures of the Madonna and Child. All of them are reverent and respectful, yet each one shows a different attitude. Like those of the children, we are moved differently by each of his paintings.

If art has psychological importance it is through depicting the psychic image. It is a psychic event. How does one measure a psychic event? The simple ritual of describing what is there—a chant telling what we see instead of our feelings about what is there, an enumeration of the parts of the image and its qualities—is one way. Although one can discover fear or joy in a child's eyes, can one measure it?

Measurement

A proponent of data-based art education once said that there are physical evidences of love—body movements that reveal the inner state—and that in evaluating an art teacher, one might count how many times the teacher smiled. "Anything can be measured," she insisted. But her argument was unconvincing. She failed to see that the qualities most important to well-being will not submit to physical measurement. It is not how many times one smiles that is important, but the quality of affection shown in each smile. It is a tragedy that so much of education and therapy are devoted to this kind of measurement when it is those things which cannot be measured that give joy and meaning to human existence. The rational approach is well equipped with rudders, but it has no musical instrument, no imagination. Ritual, not logic, constitutes the discipline of art, and to be in ritual is not simply to be blind or adrift but to see with different eyes—with an artistic instrument. Academic art education and art therapy have simply chosen the wrong instrument. Practitioners of the academic style are trying to see with the eyes of Caesar what can only be seen with the eyes of soul. They do not acknowledge that the true discipline of art is to connect with an inner image—to see ordinary things as animated personages. They do not realize that the way of life which will promote art-making and its therapeutic and educational benefits is related to the numinous self-surpassing psyche.

An aesthetic instrument is the guiding power of the psyche. It is the intuitive connection with the psychic image, and it can be encouraged by letting go of ego control and attending carefully to what cannot be anticipated, controlled, or measured. Rational thinking and ego control may develop mechanical skill, but artistic skill requires a connection with the images of one's daily experience—seeing ordinary things as animated personages. Any art-making and its therapeutic and educational benefits must recognize the numinous and artistic traditions—the self-surpassing psyche—more than logic and rational control. And it must be available to everybody.

Nature and Beauty

We have for so long thought of the earth as dead matter that it is difficult to think of the earth as alive or to realize that we help create it by participating with invisible forces. Art has been the one activity which brings us closest to such a realization. Seeing the earth anew means that we recognize the tragic drone of our common superficial attention—or lack thereof. What we first encounter is always the common. "It possesses the unearthly power to break us of the habit of abiding in what is essential."[13] It is difficult for us to pay heed because of our easy attachment to the "at first" of what is common, suggesting a real difference between the merely common and

---

[13] Martin Heidegger, *What Is Called Thinking?* Fred W. Wiek and J. Glenn Gray, trans. (New York: Harper & Row, 1968), 129.

the ordinary. An angel is necessary for us to break our attachment with the common and reach a more passionate concern. It is in his sight and hearing that we learn to see and hear the earth again.

Once again, poets have understood this. Wordsworth, through poetry, wanted to awaken "the mind's lethargy of custom,"[14] by seeing, "every common sight appareled in celestial light."[15] For Wallace Stevens it is in the angel's sight and hearing that we perceive the world. But to hear in the angel's hearing is never easy. We must acknowledge our world and respect it, and this calls for passionate concern. The passion we seek derives from the awe we will feel in facing the world as image; the power to achieve insight into a reality which we do not make or control, yet which offers a relation to the world where image is central; seeing imagination as the faculty that prevails; taking another look. Lingering in the moment of "not knowing" brings a clear image of the content of the psychic situation, thus announcing our place in the family of things. This is not a humanist point of view.

A change will be difficult. In Psyche's myth, her initiation consists of four impossible tasks which she accomplished with various helpers instead of a steering ego. Ants separate grains from the chaotic mixture. An eagle collects water from the treacherous and inaccessible peak. Not all the helpers are animals: a green reed shows her how to gather the golden fleece from fierce sheep, and a man-made tower tells her precisely how to get to the underworld and back. Beauty is the final treasure, and in order to have some of the forbidden prize for herself, Psyche opens the cask and is thrown back into a deathlike sleep. It takes passion—the love of Eros—to awaken her from the sleep of death brought about by her rational attempt to seize the prize from another realm.

This tale is about the magical or daimonic force of the unconscious imagination. Psyche is not a heroine who achieves great deeds through the strength of will and ego. Actually she is shown as a *therapeutes*—a servant to a Aphrodite, the goddess of love and beauty. The soul's essence is service to beauty. The revelation of an underworld

---

[14] Samuel Taylor Coleridge, *Biographia Literaria*, Vol. II, James Engell and W. Jackson Bates, eds. (Princeton: Princeton UP, Bollingen SeriesLXXV, 1983), 7.

[15] William Wordsworth, *English Romantic Writers*, David Perkins, ed. (New York: Harcourt Brace Janovich, Inc., 1967), 280.

psychic image awakens the heart and announces our place in the world of things—a poetic intuition half seen, "a flash of reality echoing in the world."

> And no one will ever know
> whether the picture he saw clearly
> as in a mirror, was predetermined
> by his discipline and study...
> of old lore and by his innate capacity
> for transcribing and translating
> the difficult symbols, no one will ever know how it happened
> that in a second or a second and half a second
> he saw further, saw deeper, apprehended more...[16]

Achieving clarity of image requires the aid of a sixth sense—our animal instincts—or what Cezanne called one's temperament, one's sensations before nature. It is impossible for ego and will to make the psychic image clear. They can never see it. Rational will and physical prowess are helpless to accomplish a task which is not in their realm. Cezanne, the father of modern art, spent his life working for clarity of image, and he spoke of the plurality of sensations required in art-making. The clarity he pursued with such determination and devotion cannot be achieved by a detached observer. It is not an optical clarity that he sought, but a psychological clarity. Cezanne is known to have said that painting from nature is not to copy objects, but rather to bring into being one's sensations in contact with nature.

Participation with psyche in nature is what makes the work of great painters so potent. They have felt their own energy and identi-fied with the image of external nature. They paid close attention to the world, thereby gaining the immense power that comes when the world pays attention back to them. They did not paint the outer shell of nature as an idol. Rather they sought the inner radiance or soul within nature and within everyday objects such as Cezanne's apples and Van Gogh's shoes. Cezanne saw psyche in nature. Van Gogh looked for places in nature where spirit of life was most evident. It is participation with nature which made the work of such painters so powerful. The work of art gives form or face to the invisible image.

---

[16] Hilda Doolittle, "The Flowering of the Rod," *H. D.: Collected Poems* 1912-1944, Louise L. Martz, ed. (New York: New Directions Books,1983), 607.

A passionate and careful attempt to bring the psychological image into being constitutes both the therapeutic and educational value of art-making. This invisible image can be seen only with the eyes of the soul.

What is required of the artist is to face the world as image. The work of art gives form or face to the invisible image. Art is the passionate, careful attempt to bring the image into being. Today's image may be that of the suffering object, a hellish curse, with no way back to the gods. The artist's goal is to find a way back to the gods, though like Psyche, he is bound to fail. "To be an artist is to fail as no other dare to fail." Beckett warns.[17] This echoes Keats' idea of "Negative Capability" as the quality that forms a man of "Achievement" as opposed to the man of "Power." According to Keats a man of achievement is a man "capable of being in uncertainties, mysteries, doubts, without any irritable reaching after fact and reason." Such a man "has not any individuality, any determined character,"[18] meaning that he is capable of empathy with anything, entering into it without the intrusion of his ego. The man of power, on the other hand, does have a proper self, he falls into the status of Olson's "Understanding" and "tries to make it by asserting the self as character, the self as ego."[19]

Clarity thus comes from an inner sight rather than from external sources. Art means bringing into actual form the reality of our sensations before nature. These kinds of sensations do not arise from our five physical sense organs. They come from the psyche which uses the senses. And they cannot be instilled through rational arguments or technical instruction. Images are shaped by forces which are mysterious and beyond our will. They do not follow rules, principles or convention. We can only help the patient or student to develop the necessary insight to see psychologically and develop the patience and determination to honor the image. The teacher or therapist must help the artist get in touch with the image, not only with the physical appearance of the object. "How do you feel about this object or subject matter?" may be too blunt and abstract, but a dialogue about the

[17] Samuel Beckett, *Samuel Beckett: Poet and Critic*, Lawrence E. Harvey, ed. (Princeton: Princeton UP, 1970), 434.

[18] John Keats, "Letter to George and Tom Keats, December, 1817," *Letters of John Keats*, Robert Gittings, ed. (Oxford: Oxford UP, 1979), 43.

[19] Charles Olson, *The Special View of History: Notes from Black Mountain, 1956* (Berkeley: Oyez, 1970), 16.

subject matter and what is your part in it will give us better answers to that question. In discussing one's part in a situation, one becomes involved in the action and the objects. It becomes a story or a drama. Feelings and emotions spontaneously arise.

We cannot really help the patient or student if our attention is focused on how they should be expressing themselves. It is not knowledge about technique that is of first importance. In speaking about an academic art exam, Marion Richardson says,

> Given the ability to imitate outward physical appearances it was no doubt assumed that students would one day achieve the power to paint something of their own. The fact is that not one in a hundred ever dreamt of doing so. The language was not theirs so that even if they could speak it, they would say nothing.[20]

Academic approaches are based on the false assumption that the object is the image and thus requires an optical perception. Yet what we appreciate in art is not its likeness to nature but rather the glimpse we get into the nature of essential reality, whether or not it presents a photographic likeness. We frequently see a reproduction of a Cezanne landscape placed next to a photograph of the scene that was his "motif." The greater vitality in the painting is striking compared to the photograph. We appreciate the psychological image as seen through a temperament and a sense of the living breath or *aesthesis*. What makes art education a vital experience and makes art therapy therapeutic is the cultivation of this aesthetic sense. When we struggle to clarify our sensations and inner images, then we experience the therapy of art in a deep and significant way. If we approach images as problems or diseases that we must eradicate, how can we expect to gain any understanding?

It is easy to forget that at the time he painted them, Cezanne's works were considered crude, primitive, violent, and the work of an "insane man." When artists first began depicting inner images rather than the outer face of nature, their work was not understood. And this is, at least partly, because things have been abused. The abuse of things deserves our attention as much as does the abuse of children.

---

[20] Marion Richardson, *Art and the Child* (London: London UP, 1948), 17.

The world's disorders are man-made projections of our own subjectivity, denying subjectivity to the objects we manipulate.

Psyche once had a place in the world and was seen in the face of nature. However by the eighteenth century, such seeing was labeled "animism" and discredited. We see what our ideas allow us to see and when a culture begins to believe that nature is merely dead soulless matter, the artist has to take up the cause of psyche and look beyond the outer face of nature to expose her inner reality, to produce images that will animate our emotions. The soul was driven inward by the enlightenment and science. When psyche is driven inward the gods become symptoms.

The World is Sick

It is up to art therapists and educators to pursue paths that seem unclear, crude, and unscientific. In a materialist soulless society, clarity will require that we allow the coarse and violent images to come forth as well as those that are pleasing and harmonious. "For there, in a black pause, strange textured figures and images force us to acknowledge their otherness, and in their otherness lives the soul."[21] A black and violent image does not necessarily mean that the artist has a black and violent intention. The artist does not control these inner guests. Nor does a black and violent image necessarily indicate a patient's sickness or perversity. The world is sick. The soul is larger than any individual and larger than humankind. It is the nonphysical aspect of all nature, including mankind. Soul is in both the artist and the object produced. There is a faculty in mankind which is capable of perceiving in an aesthetic sense the nonphysical relations which underlie creation, and it is this faculty which produces art. When our images deny the reality of the soul, the soul may have to produce violent and black images to shock us into accepting the idea that there is a reality beyond our ken, and into paying attention to the world. Artists who hear the cry of the objective psyche and who paint dark images are not necessarily sick or depraved. They may be hearing the "tragic drone" of the earth's "stiff and stubborn man-locked set." They may be hearing the cry of the *anima mundi*.

---

[21] Mary A. Doll, *Beckett and Myth: An Archetypal Approach* (Syracuse: Syracuse UP, 1988), 7.

Classifications that are found in the diagnostic manual DSM-4 repeat the taxonomic eye and the prescriptive formula for cure rather than the psychological eye and the mythical mode of poetic precision required for art-making and soul-making. In art education the move toward a data-based art education is a backward move toward a belief in a material cause, which even the latest developments in modern physics can no longer claim as self-evident. Materialistic cause and effect assumptions ignore the mystery and limitless depth of both art and psyche.

It is particularly difficult to see soul in things we have habitually seen with mundane or sentimental eyes. It is a mistake to think of the experience of the *anima mundi* as extraordinary. All of life is governed by archetypal patterns which are the voice of the world soul. This is the great paradox which gives a universal dimension to our individual thoughts and experiences. There is a faculty in humankind which is capable of perceiving esthetically the archetypal grids that underlie our existence. Hillman writes:

> These grids are more like contour maps of the imagination which allow the mind to read itself imaginatively; whereas explanations are more like bulldozers that flatten the imagination's terrain into plain thinking useful for conceptual constructs. Call these engraved lines archetypes, call them mythical grids, call them imaginal persons or ideational forms. Whatever they be named, they are to be distinguished from the categories that philosophers like Aristotle and Kant held to be basic mental structures: abstract categories like space and time, motion, and number. Mythical grids are figurative and personified. They are found most easily in the arts (drama, painting, sculpture, and poetry).[22]

They are personified in the gods and goddesses. In an age of transition like ours, it gives these figures dramatic vitality to see them personified as divine.

Each image is unique and each archetype is complex. To generalize the uniqueness of the image to its easily classified mythical pattern may provide a false security. Seeing the mythic grids is necessary to

---

[22] James Hillman, *Kinds of Power* (New York: Current Doubleday, 1995), 219-20.

connect to our mythological origins, and we may find healing in the power of the mythical figures. Lockhart wrote of the need to see the details:

> [I]n the same way that we often tend to overlook the intimate details of a mythic story by pulling out only a thread or two from an interwoven fabric, we likewise overlook many of the details of imagery that are unrecognizable in the pattern and unique in their quality. Typically we are easily attracted to the details of imagery that can be readily comprehended. What gets overlooked and quickly forgotten is the fine and subtle detail that is unique. Yet one's exact fate and individuality are tied to those details.[23]

Psychological sensitivity does not bring scientific understanding. It does not produce useful knowledge or solve practical problems. But it does recognize the *anima mundi* and promote sensitivity to the world of things and events.

We can reanimate the ordinary and avoid sentimental and romantic wish fulfillment, through a recognition of the numinous power of myth as an archetypal paradigm for the psychic events in our lives. That is how we keep reality alive. Myths are an older and richer way of knowing reality in its ordinary immediate sensuous presentation. Myths present the collective experience of a society. Through myth, seen as metaphor, we reexperience the life of the group. Through art work, seen as metaphor, we can experience with patients or students their psychological situation and relate this to collective myths, and by relating this to collective myths, meaning is amplified.

---

[23] Russell Lockhart, *Psyche Speaks: A Jungian Approach to Self and World* (Wilmette, Ill.: Chiron Publications, 1987), 54.

IV

CARE ENOUGH

The desire to see and the need to be seen cannot be over-
estimated; when such seeing and being seen take place it is
like a blessing.

—James Hillman

In the front rank of researchers into the mysteries of self-
surpassing stands the artist—the professional of
inspiration, who proves himself by material evidences of
his capacity to see and create. His trade goes back to the
oracles and soothsayers of ancient civilizations, yet society sees in him the figure of an avant-guard able to offer
insights into truths so far inaccessible... Is not inspiration—that state of magically heightened capacity—with
him a matter of everyday necessity?

—Harold Rosenberg

Emotions are the theme of earthly life. They come to us un-
bidden and hold us in their grip. They determine our moods
and behavior, and we are motivated to express our emotions
by their urgent insistence. Our third principle, "care enough," relies
on "making a match between an emotional experience and a form
that has been conceived but not created."[1]

Art is symbolic in that it tells what is otherwise inexpressible. This is
the truth of psychological knowing and of imagination. It is a telling
of subtle truths. As a teller of truth the artist must not only see clearly

---

[1] Clive Bell, *The Artistic Problem Since Cezanne* (Freeport, New York: Books for
Libraries Press, 1969), 43.

but this seeing must motivate creativity. The artist, then, must take over the role of soothsayer. In such a time inspiration becomes an everyday necessity. Everyone of us, then, must be an artist.

The image-making power of the autonomous psyche is not the work of human will and reason. Instead it is mysterious and numinous. In our secular age we have become unconscious of these psychic images, even though ordinary things are permeated by the uninvited images presented by psyche. Only when we dwell in the twilight realms of the unconscious psyche can we realize (through art, in this case) the value of ordinary things. This is imagining the archetypal.

When a student or patient begins to "daub" or to "fix up" a picture, it is often a sign that the fire has gone out, that the angel is no longer being attended. It is at this point that the emotional connection has been severed, and it is the artist's constant job to reestablish the connection.

> [The artist] will need a definite fully conceived form into which his experience can be made to fit. And this fitting, this match of his experience with this form will be his problem. It will be at once a canal and a goad. And his energy and intellect between them will have to keep warm his emotion.
>
> Only, to be satisfactory, the problem must be for him who employs it a goad and a limitation, a goad that calls forth all his energies; a limitation that focuses them on some object far more precise and comprehensible than the expression of a vague sensibility. For the artistic problem, which limits the artist's freedom, fixes his attention on a point, and drives his emotion through narrow tubes, is what imports the conventional element into art.[2]

It takes a certain amount of intensity, even passion, to "expand the bosom of God." An emotional push may be required for us to see the vision with precision and to move psyche to a deeper connection with the world, to see the gods in everyday things. This push can come in the form of an epiphany, a manifestation or appearance of a divine being. However, Blake saw that "some good we may do when the man is in a passion, but no good when the passion is in the man." Hillman expands this idea to include the idea of epiphany:

---

[2] *Op. cit.*, 44.

Figure 1

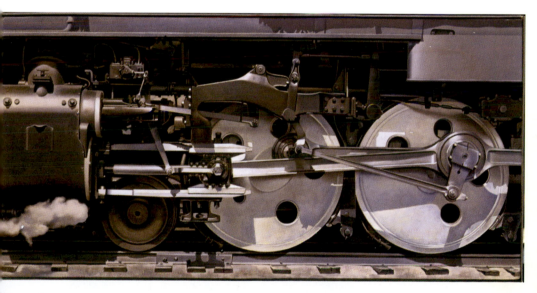

Figure 2

Figure 3

Figure 4

Figure 5

Figure 6

Figure 7

Figure 8

Figure 9  Figure 10

Figure 11

Figure 12

Figure 13

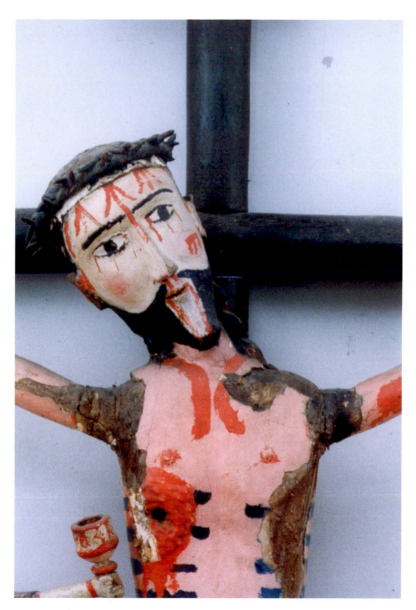

Figure 14

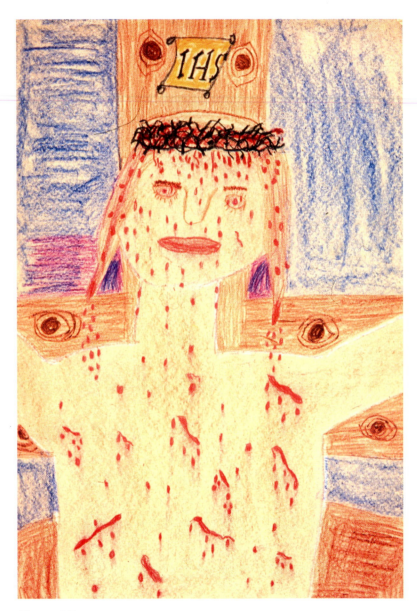

Figure 15

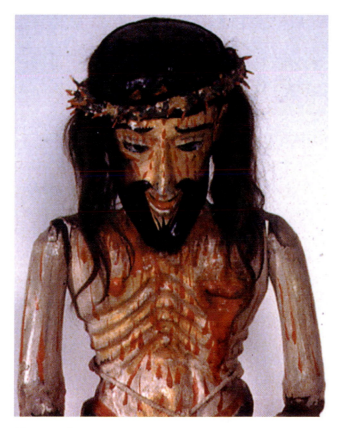

Figure 16

Figure 17

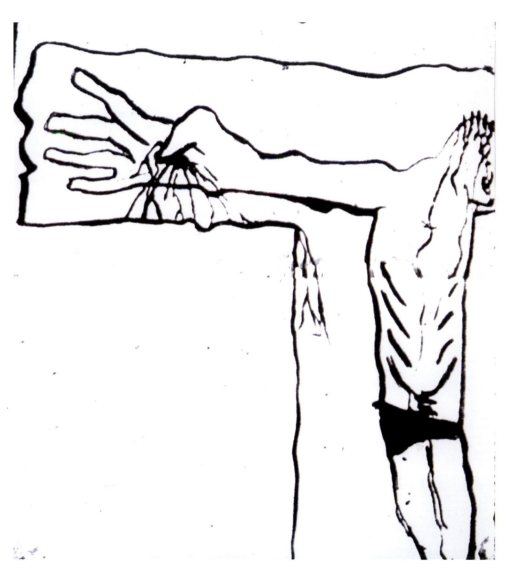

Figure 18

Figure 19

Figure 20

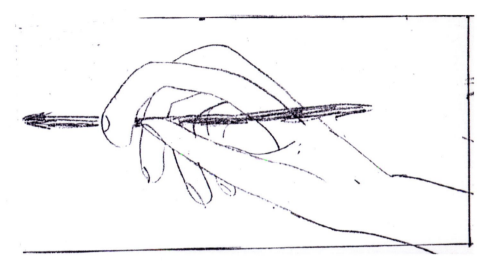

Figure 21

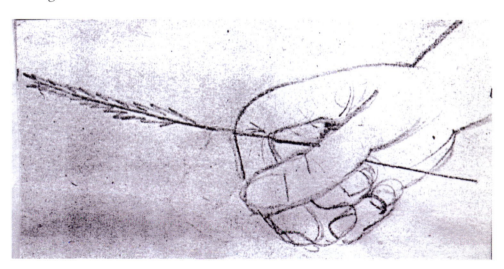

Figure 23

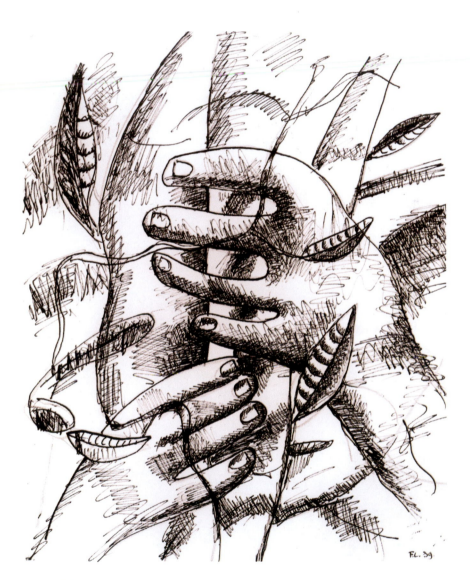

Figure 22

> To have passion in me is demonic; to be in a passion, in the
> world of emotions, and grasped by the way it signifies all
> things with a specific vision or insight, may move the psyche
> to a deeper and epiphanic connection within the world.[3]

Connecting one's daily experience with one's inner image, seeing
ordinary things as animated images, paying close attention, caring
enough, and giving the image a concrete form will make the invisible
visible. To encourage close attention to the artistic problem requires
something different from the teaching of anatomy, proportion, perspective, and principles of design, and color harmony. Instead it is
necessary for patients and students to forget such rules and principles and remember their image—what first inspired them to begin
the drawing. Sometimes careful reflection on the work as a drawing
in process will enliven the passion and get the artist started again. Or
a specific difficulty may demand the attention and energy of eros—a
change to an unfamiliar medium or a clumsy instrument for example.
(I sometimes ask a student or patient to attach a brush or piece of
charcoal to the end of a yardstick and draw standing with the paper
placed on the wall or the floor.)

Art is generated by an emotional impulse. It is a genuine response
to one's reality, a means of communication with the world and with
life. It requires an intense encounter.

> To come face-to-face with the earth not as a conglomera-
> tion of physical fact, but in the person of its angel is an
> essential psychic event which can "take place" neither in
> the world of impersonal abstract concepts nor on the plane
> of sensory data. The earth has to be perceived not by the
> senses, but through a primordial image, and inasmuch as
> image comes with the features of a personal figure, it will
> prove to "symbolize with" the very image of itself which
> the soul carries in its innermost depth.[4]

It is a passionate, even desperate, acknowledgment of the tragedy of
the world today, our neglect of soul, that gives a need for a principle
that asks us to "care enough." Art therapists and art educators must

---

[3] James Hillman, *Emotion: A Comprehensive Phenomenology of Theories and their
Meanings for Therapy* (Evanston, Ill.: Northwestern UP, 1992), x.

[4] Henry Corbin, *Spiritual Body and Celestial Earth* (Princeton: Princeton UP,
Bollingen Series XCI 2, 1977), 4.

that asks us to "care enough." Art therapists and art educators must nurture such intensity.

One young male student was passionately involved with religious concerns. He was seeking self-conformation in this age of transition (and his own transition from adolescence to manhood). The image that struck him was the wounded hands of Christ, pierced and bleeding. He wrote a number of poems about this martyrdom. One, entitled "Crucifixion," spoke of those who looked on as Christ died.

> His swollen finger tries
>
> as blood drips, and drips
> beautiful red, am, but he is right.
>
> They watch as His head hangs lower…
> they with tears in their eye.
>
> And then it seems as if He smiles between the tears
> for he knows they are sorry.
>
> Then it is time to die.
>
> They walk, and they look, but mostly they walk.

His adolescent poems and the accompanying pictures seemed to be the passionate expression of the world's tragedy as well as of his drive toward individual self-discovery. His drawings (**figs. 17-20**), only a few examples of many he did) may seem to be lacking in skill, but the improvement that is evident in them was crafted by his passion to find the proper shape for his image. The figures he drew in response to his image of the crucified Christ clearly indicate the intensity and sincerity of his feelings. One can see the concentrated effort in the persistence shown in the series of drawings. The bleeding hands were the emotional focus for this young man, and here his image becomes clearer.

Clarity of visual thinking is essential for learning a new way of looking. Developing this new way of looking is essential to art therapists and art educators if they want art-making to be a blessing and not just an exercise in skill. Even "clarity" needs to be thought of in a new way. "Clear" does not necessarily mean logical or rational thinking. It can also imply a psychological or imaginal clarity. As opposed to a discursive certitude, an imaginal clarity is not a one and naked truth.

In order to gain such clarity we must give up the belief that we are separate from nature, that only humans have soul and only humans can make decisions. We must, at the very least, admit, along with many modern physicists, that we are a part of a much larger organism, the earth, or possibly even the universe. We share soul with the rest of existence and, like the *augures* we can see with the eyes of the soul.

If the word "psyche" means "soul" we may gain some insight into seeing with the eyes of the soul by attending more closely to the myth of Psyche. When Psyche disobeys Amor (Eros) and looks upon him with the eyes of flesh, he flees from her. Likewise if we cannot see in students' or clients' work the psychic reality which they are struggling to express, if we concentrate our attention on teaching skill in the use of materials or on realistic representation of subject matter, the image will flee and we will have to begin again our initiation into the underworld. Only that poetic intuition which is the psychic image can keep the work of soul-making alive.

Like Psyche, who is persuaded by her worldly sisters to look upon Eros, most clients and students are persuaded by our materialistic viewpoint that art-making means realistic representation of a story, or subjective expression of a personal emotion. Promoting clarity of psyche's view requires that art therapists and teachers promote an oracular, imaginal way of looking. The blessing of "self-surpassing" is proven by the artist's capacity to see in the tradition of the oracles and soothsayers with an imagination that comes through the psyche or soul. Such self-surpassing means to experience oneself "through the third faculty of the psyche." Seeing with the eyes of the soul starts from within the imaginal itself. Both education and therapy require self-surpassing and this only happens when we touch the soul of the world, the *anima-mundi*. We can only surpass ourselves when we open up to the depths of the human psyche. Such opening up is not an objective observing. It is a feeling, a sensing, with the inspiration of the *augures*, a shadow seeing with the eyes of the soul.

Perhaps this sense of the shadow is the first clue to the clarity we seek. We do not create the images we paint or sculpt, we find them. We find them if we learn to see as *augures*, and if our ego can let go of the desire to rule. Enter here initiation through ritual—finding a time and a place for attending to what is happening.

Art Therapy and Traditional Clinics

It is easy to understand why art therapists and art educators would be tempted to adjust to the demands of disinterested research and promote "disciplined" imagination to prove to society that art teaching or art therapy are serious areas of intellectual study and practice. There is pressure for art therapists and educators to gain acceptance and prove to the ego-centered culture that our work is serious. But while these professions are serious, intellectual fields of study, they employ different tools. Diagnostic systems like the "House-Tree-Person" test, the Kinetic Family Drawings, and the DSM-4 are rudders of the steering ego which offer plausibility and credibility in a society more concerned with normalcy and statistical measurements than with psychological understanding of the fantasy image. The tools and theories of our materialistic society do not validate the worth of the individual, and our language is foreign to them.

Art therapists and educators who use unconventional tools and feel misunderstood are not alone. Jung, who first brought mandalas to the attention of psychology, also grew frustrated with how some viewed his work:

> When anybody who expects to be taken seriously is deluded enough to think that... I get my patients whenever possible to draw mandalas for the purpose of bringing them to the "right point," then I really must protest and tax these people with having read my writings with the most horrible inattention.[5]

Art therapists and educators must accept that in our power-driven society they will lack power. But while we lack the authority of science, we hold the authority of art. We must acknowledge that authority and nurture it and give up hope of power and riches in a materialist, consumer society. But this acknowledgment must come without diminishing our motivation or our intensity for our work.

If aesthetic perception is imagination, then we can easily see its importance for art education and art therapy. We must also realize that, based as it is on the poetical faculty, art therapy offers a unique

[5] C. G. Jung, *Psychology and Alchemy*, *CW 12* (Princeton: Princeton UP, Bollingen Series, XX., 1968), § 126.

dimension for both hospital and clinic. Art therapy, being distinct from medicine's regular *modus operandi*, offers an addition to their repertory of therapeutic modes. This is its only purpose in these institutions: art therapy does not compete with medical or physical therapies. It brings a unique dimension to the clinic, and it is for this reason alone that art therapy is valuable there.

Since the scientific revolution in the seventeenth century, science has defined reality as physical existence. And because such a view assumed that all reality was in some way physical, any idea having to do with the nonphysical reality of psyche was discredited. Emotions were assumed to come either from chemical reactions in the body or brain or from learned reactions from the environment. Everything that was not measurable in terms of physical matter was suspect. However when quantum mechanics discovered that even physical reality is based on the viewers perspective rather than objective physical fact, that particular scientific view collapsed. Now the scientist and the archetypal psychologist can agree that basic reality cannot be reached in any direct way through the senses. The basic stuff of matter (even if you are only considering physical reality) cannot be seen, touched, smelled, or heard. It can only be assumed to exist via our observations of the results.

The subatomic particle is no more substantial than the psyche. Both are models we have developed to explain our experiences to ourselves. Steven Hawking, the eminent theoretical physicist, tells us that "a scientific theory is just a mathematical model which we make to describe our observations" and "may initially be put forward for aesthetic or metaphysical reasons."[6] In speaking of time Hawking says: "So it is meaningless to ask: Which is real, 'real' or 'imaginary' time? It is simply a matter of which is the more useful description."[7] For psychotherapy the imaginal is the more useful because image is the realm of the psyche as it is the realm of art.

Too often we are blinded by our desire to see—to grasp reality with our senses—just as Tiresias was blinded for wanting to see Athena (But Tiresias was then given a new kind of vision. He became a seer.)

---

[6] Steven W. Hawking, *A Brief History of Time: From Big Bang to Black Holes* (Toronto: Bantam Books, 1998), 136-37.
[7] *Ibid.*, 139.

Too often we confuse imaginal with subjective and internal, and we mistake essential for external and objective. We cannot see with the eyes of the soul if we are focused on external reality and we may miss the archetypal image if we believe that the art work reflects only that which is personal.

Classifications that are found in the DSM-4 use the taxonomic eye to justify a prescriptive formula for cure. But it is a psychological eye and mythical mode of precision that is required for art-making. The move toward a data-based art education is a backward move toward a belief in a material cause, which even the latest developments in modern physics can no longer claim as self-evident. Materialistic cause-and-effect assumptions ignore the mystery and limitless depth of both art and psyche. It is particularly difficult to see with the eyes of the soul things which we have habitually seen with mundane or sentimental eyes.

To desire to establish art therapy on a scientific or clinical base—rather than on an aesthetic or imaginal base—is an anomaly. Archetypal psychology seems to be the only psychology that fully appreciates the role of images in human perception and expression. We must personify in order to recognize the archetypal figures in our individual modes of functioning. The archetypal removes our functioning from ego control. A dominant ego blocks our vision of images. Archetypal psychology and the rhetorical perspective conceive resemblance vertically. Images and objects are linked back to their paradigmatic archetypal origins. Objects and those who live with them are seen through the image in which they were created. The gods are visible.

The diagnostic perspective, on the other hand, conceives differences horizontally, as opposites. People and objects are compared to others with similar traits. Individuals are classified. A norm is sought and often established. The horizontal view identifies patients and their art work with what is not unique in them: they are no longer seen as the image which they embody. What is unique in a person becomes a problem requiring diagnosis and interpretation rather than an incomparable attribution in need of affection. Art eductors and art therapists can—and perhaps must—help schools and clinics to see this difference.

The Face of the Invisible

From the point of view of scientific analysis, the ego is strengthened, and imagination is seen as a weakness. The principle at hand, "care enough," depends on a relationship between the artist and the world which allows for the mysterious and the numinous. It calls for an intensity of devotion to the image, a passionate concern inspired by the angel, god, or goddess revealed in the image. We must care enough to see the face of the invisible essence of the objects and events of our daily experience. It means, as Cezanne suggested, transforming one's sensations before nature into the rhythms of one's temperament, of psyche's sensibilities. The animal instinct is more effective in art than rational conception, as is soul before ego. The "what" is the ordinary things and experiences, and the "who" are the archetypal persons to which all our actions and ideas may be traced back. This is done through epistrophe.

The imaginal universe exists before all our conscious projects and determines them, as Henry Corbin, a scholar of Islamic mysticism, suggests. The imaginal universe is not an illusory realm nor is it a concrete idea preceding the act of creation. "For it is from the soul itself, from the 'celestial Earth' of the soul, that the 'spiritual flesh' is constituted—the supra-sensory and at the same time perfectly concrete *cara spiritualis*."[8] The imaginal universe is that place from whence come the figures of our imagination. It is prior to our conscious awareness and it shapes the world we inhabit. It governs our daily lives. Corbin explains that the world in question "cannot be perceived by the organ of ordinary knowledge; that it can be neither proven nor disputed by means of ordinary argumentation, that it is a world so different that it can neither be seen nor perceived except by the organ of 'Hurqalyan' perception."[9] Hurqalya is Islamic imagination, the "celestial Earth" of aesthetic perception.

This invisible is a reality so different that it cannot be seen or perceived except by the imagination:

---

[8] Henry Corbin, *Spiritual Body and Celestial Earth: From Mazdean Iran to Shi'ite Iran* (Princeton: Princeton UP, Bollingen Series XCI 2, 1977), ix and xii, respectively.
[9] *Ibid.*, xii.

> I believe it will seem very strange to the historian of the
> future, that a literal minded generation began to accept
> the actuality of a "collective unconscious" before it could
> even admit the possibility of a "collective conscious" in
> the shape of the phenomenal world.[10]

This idea of a real but invisible world was also introduced to the
world of physics by physicist Niels Bohr. What Bohr called "prob-
ability waves," Heisenberg called, "a strange kind of physical reality
just in the middle between possibility and reality"This real but invisible world is the world of images, and it is from this world that the
artist must get his vision. It is the experience of this world that makes
the art process educational as well as therapeutic.

Artistic seeing is an emotional response to the image. There is no
scientific or systematic measurement. In teaching rules of proportion or design we neglect the fact that out images are shaped by forces
that are mysterious and beyond the will. We can develop such insight
if we are willing to let go of ego control, if we are willing to be
moved by the angel of reality, the angelic in the ordinary. On the
other hand if we believe that there is no reality except the psychical
world, we will be unable to hear the angel's message. We will rush in
with instructions of how to do it "right." The first step, then is to
have an open mind to the possibility that there is an invisible world
which can speak to us. We must then be patient and allow something
unexpected to happen. The art therapist or teacher must have faith
and patience as well as the sensitivity to see, hear, and be moved. The
"help" we give comes from insight into our own suffering as a result
of our empathic response to the suffering of the world.

Archetypal Psychology

Sensitivity of this kind initiates "one person creeds" based on personal experience in its unique form. It is a revolt against tradition
and convention. Archetypal psychology, too, is a revolt against tradition. It seeks additional structures and broader myths. Daily
experiences and images no longer need to be condemned as wrong or

---

[10] Owen Barfield, *Saving the Appearances: A Study in Idolatry* (New York: Harbin-
ger, not dated), 135.

once we have discovered their archetypal foundations. Thus the images are just as they should be. It is up to us to learn how to see them in a psychological light.

Archetypal psychology is based on the principle that all phenomena have an archetypal likeness—such as gods and goddesses—to which they can be related. This is the principle of epistrophe. Our psychological lives are mimetic to myths, and in this way therapy can be seen as the study of the stories of the soul. Each insight corresponds to archetypal patterns which are the primary material of human life, recorded in myths, fairy tales, and lore. Our personal experiences are in themselves secondary experiences which can be reverted to the primary background of the archetype. The task of art therapy and art education is to try to discover these archetypal patterns for the forms of behavior and the images we observe.

> The assumption is always that *everything belongs somewhere*: all forms of psychopathology have their mythical substrate and belong or have their home in myths. Moreover, psychopathology is itself a means of reverting to myth; a means of being affected by myth and entering into a myth. Or as Jung said, "The gods have become diseases." So that today it is to our pathologies that we must look for finding the Gods. [11]

Rather than analysis the main work of psychotherapy is epistrophe—as Hillman puts it, "for us it is the conservation and exploration and vivification of the imagination, and the insights derived therefrom" rather than the analysis of the unconscious" that is the goal. [12] We must care fervently enough to appreciate the necessity of the image.

The Passion of the Gods

This returns us to emotions in the principle of "care enough." As modern art has shown, the vivification of imagination requires an anxious—even desperate—application of insight. Such intensity

---

[11] James Hillman, "Pothos: The Nostalgia of the Puer Eternus," *Loose Ends: Primary Papers in Archetypal Psychology* (Zürich: Spring Publications, 1975), 50.
[12] *Ibid.*

is a result of our longing, a restless urge which cannot find its object, a yearning for a distant and unattainable goal. This archetypal longing is personified by the god Pothos, who is associated with the *puer aeternus* and is, with Aphrodite, one of the main figures of the ancient mystery cult of Samothrace. Pothos is an aspect of eros, love's spiritual component—the erotic component of spirit—or passion.

The young Pothos is portrayed on a fifth century Greek vase drawing Aphrodite's chariot, an indicator that beauty must be carried by passion. Pothos can be seen as the motivation driving the desire, a striving power connected with love and beauty. The longing is for truth representing the propensity to learn. It is excessive, uneasy, never satisfied. The passion is extravagant and resourceful—passion reaches out to passion. This is the heart that lies at the center of art therapy and education. It is the necessary angel.

It is not the goal of art education to satisfy the intellect, nor is it the goal of art therapy to heal self-division. (Each of us consists of multiple archetypal persons.) Rather the goal of both is to reflect and acknowledge yearning and to encourage passion. Yearning and passion can become helpful guides in one's life and can lead to new insights and achievements. Being open to such passion can be a form of initiation into a world of imagination. This initiation will not provide a compass for single-minded direction, but rather an instrument to stir emotions. Our yearning is for an image that will stir our passion. Personal experience is reflected back to its universal archetypal source. This initiation of the hungry heart is only attainable through imagination, the exuberant excess of unnecessary wants.

Harold Rosenberg has taken interest in the individual statement of the anxious, even desperate, artist. He concludes that society is moving toward a point when personal experience will be the foundation of culture and its expressions.

> Today art consists of one-person creeds; one-psyche cultures. Its direction is toward a society in which the experience of each will be the ground of a unique inimitable form—in short, a society in which everyone will be an artist. Art in our time can have no other social aim...[13]

---

[13] Harold Rosenberg, "Metaphysical Feelings in Modern Art," *Critical Inquiry* (2, 1975), 231.

Here lies the root of interest in the art work of children and untrained adults. Here, too, is the validation for art education in public schools and for art as a mode of therapy.

Modern art, revolting against the Renaissance traditions of representation and harmony, turned to dissonant and distorted modes of expression which can also be found in the art of "primitive" peoples and children. Aesthetic perception—and the five principles which follow it—allows us to see value in idiosyncratic expression and the psychological value of "one-person creeds." But to avoid domination by tradition and to produce unique and inimitable forms, one must let the psyche speak in and through the work.

The Voice of Psyche in Practice

Using a scientific or medical model gives art therapists and educators a false sense of security. Such methods are wrong for art therapy and education not because science and medicine are wrong but because they tend to place art in an alien field. When we submit to the demands of insurance companies which make demands foreign to our work, then we are succumbing to the ills of our manic consumer society and its desire for the speed and efficiency of an industrial machine. We could even be perpetuating the very trauma which brings patients to therapy.

To try to fit into a scientific model is going over to another order. It is ugly! Art therapy requires different skills and a different orientation. We must care enough about our calling to resist temptation to give ourselves over to the other order, which would be to deny our authenticity and lose the authority inherent in art.

How might we motivate our patients to seek inspiration from their world? There are no set techniques ready at hand to help a patient gain the inspiration necessary to create a work of art, and the processes of one therapist will almost always vary from that of another. One way to help, which has already been suggested, is to encourage patients to pay close attention to the world of things and experiences. Another way is to help the patient get in touch with where they are emotionally and psychically at the present moment. This can be achieved by asking the patient to bring an autobiographical sketch to the second therapy session. I like to ask for information about parents and grandparents too since, as poet Rainer Maria Rilke said, "much stands behind me."

Poetry can be an inspiration, even for patients who are usually not "into" poetry. When the poem has relevance, it speaks to the patient's concerns. After telling a patient not to worry about their ability to draw—"Your psyche will help you, and your fingers will know what to do"—I often read a poem by Rilke which helps to start the patient thinking about our loss of touch with the animal sense.

> My life is not this steeply flowering hour
> In which you see me hurrying.
> Much stands behind me,
> I stand before it like a tree
> And I am only one of many.
>
> I am the rest between two notes
> Which are always in discord
> Because death's note wants to climb over.
>
> And in the dark, eternal, reconciled,
> They stay there, trembling.
>
> And the song goes on, beautiful. [14]

This poem begins the discussion that patients are not the surface rush and bustle, not these superficial concerns and worries, because much stands behind them. We do not know what stands before us, or how long it will be. The important thing is that what stands behind us gives us grounding. Coming to terms with the present is at the same time discovering a connection between past and future. Now what is this trembling—the trembling between two discordant notes, between past and future? If you can get in touch with that trembling, the song will go on. And it will be beautiful.

---

[14] Rainer Maria Rilke, *Selected Poems of Rainer Maria Rilke*, Robert Bly, trans. (New York: Harper & Row, 1981), 31.

V

NEVER GENERALIZE

> Skill aims at making beauty, or letting beauty appear, because this both stops the whirling dislocated soul from thrashing around and gives pleasure to the soul and makes the world pleasing.
>
> —*James Hillman*

> There are no techniques at anyone's disposal for saying what he has to say. He has no proof of his authority or genuineness, other than his own work... Each work requires a new step.
>
> —*Stanley Cavell*

Each thing is unique as it presents itself. The fourth principle, "never generalize," is designed to encourage students and patients to look carefully at things in the world, notice how each one is different, and hold the image in memory as they work. This is a psychological looking. It evokes the life of the object. When one looks with the spiritual eye the object of one's vision is activated and made pregnant with possibility.

The English verb "to look" does not convey this meaning, but the German verb *betrachten* means both to look at and to be pregnant. In a deeper sense, then concentrating one's attention on an object activates it. Looking carefully means looking with a spiritual eye, seeing each object as an active force. The craft in art-making is to look at the world psychologically, making the object look back at us. Only then does the object appear.

Memory and Psychological Seeing

Psychological seeing not only activates the object, it also evokes the best of ourselves, including the necessary craftsmanship to craft the image that calls us to art (not necessarily in a Renaissance representational style, but not ruling out representational styles). It is a process of emptying the rational mind in order to receive what consciousness will not volunteer—"The best of our many selves...the fine essence of a smothered divinity."[1] Therein is the craft which will teach the hand to perform its artistry. The world paying attention back to you is pregnant with image. Being true to oneself is where beauty is found. Samuel Beckett calls this kind of seeing, "involuntary memory."[2]

The original meaning of the word "memory" is "the gathering of the constant intention of everything that the heart holds present in being," and that intention is, "the inclination with which the inmost meditation of the heart turns toward all that is in being."[3] It is a kind of pregnant seeing that results from involuntary memory, activates the object, and awakens the best in ourselves. Aesthetic perception is the basis of this craft. "Out of memory and within memory the soul pours forth its wealth of images.[4]

This meditation of the heart is what Schaefer-Simmern means when he says that the only instruction necessary is to work as slowly as possible. For him, even after the drawing is "complete," an artist should take a step back and look again. This is not to overwork the drawing but rather to encourage a heightened sense of seeing.

> After completing the drawing observe it at length, if the outline is not clear enough, fill it in with black ink to make a silhouette in order to see the object more clearly, and whenever a change seems to be necessary, start a new drawing.[5]

---

[1] Samuel Beckett in *Beckett and Myth* by Mary Doll (Syracuse: Syracuse UP, 1988), 11.

[2] This is a term Beckett used in *Proust* as a precondition to artistic creation. It was a process of emptying the mind's known rational contents so as to receive what consciousness would not volunteer, "the best of our many selves... the fine essence of a smothered divinity." See Doll, 11.

[3] Martin Heidegger, *What is Called Thinking?* (New York: Harper & Row, 1968), 141.

[4] *Ibid.*, 140.

[5] Henry Schaefer-Simmern, *The Unfolding of Artistic Activity* (Berkeley: The University of California Press, 1948), 73.

In other words do not try to fix what the rational mind wants fixed but start over and let the drawing emerge. Craft demands a slowing down of the "whirling dislocated soul," a psychological seeing, and a genuine involvement. Psychological seeing depends upon paying close attention to the world, allowing the object to magnify. The root of all craft lies in this involuntary memory—the gathering of the constant intention of what the heart holds.

If memory is the mother of the muses, then its relation to aesthetics is obvious. It is made evident by the heart's perception of everything that exists, things as they present themselves to the heart, where care, passion, and love reside. Art presents a formed emotion. The heart's meditation is what perception is all about. This is the aesthetic awareness of Aphrodite's ubiquitous presence in well crafted things. This is more than our usual ideas of beauty which often consider only pretty or pleasing and harmonious things to be beautiful. Beauty resides in the world of sense perception rather than some heavenly "prettiness" or sentimentality. If we posses beauty then we are true to our own being, as we have already posited, then craft would mean being true to one's self. Beauty resides in ordinary objects and is perceived by our spiritual eye. The world of objects is beautiful if we do not becloud it with concepts, which would be to go over to another order. It does not matter whether it is joy or grief we are experiencing, its image can be magnificent when presented aesthetically.

This idea of being true to one's self, with its rejection of concepts and scientific order does not mean that it is irrational. On the contrary it is only rational to be true to oneself. Heidegger puts it in philosophical terms:

> Reason is the perception of what is, which means also what can be and what ought to be. To perceive implies, in ascending order: to welcome and take in; to accept and take in the encounter; to take up face to face; to understand and see through—and this means to talk through. The Latin for talking through is *reor* the Greek *pew* (as in rhetoric) is the ability to take up something and see it through; *reri* is "ratio"; *animale rationale* is the animal which lives by perceiving what is...[6]

---

[6] Martin Heidegger, *op. cit.*, 61.

If we think of reason this way we can begin to understand craft as not less disciplined or less skillful, but demanding a different discipline and skill. It is like having a conversation with the object or experience, welcoming it, taking in the encounter, taking it in face to face, and thus being true to its essential nature as well as to our own. We can recognize the divinity in the image.

In this kind of discipline there is no ineffectual retreat into the lovely and etheric. Instead beauty means facing what is there before our eyes, before our heart, coming to know it, welcoming it, accepting it, and talking to it. This is a stronger and deeper sense of beauty, and it is the basis of our ability to craft the image. We cannot make what we do not perceive aesthetically. We cannot welcome, take in, and see through what does not enter the heart. Craft, in this sense, is a meditation, a careful observation that demands slowing down in order that our psychological eye may activate the object of our vision. It means submission of the ego to a god or goddess—a submission that our modern worship of materialistic and intellectual ways of knowing have not allowed.

Craft can be related to aesthetic perception through Aphrodite whose beauty lies in the ordinary objects we meet in our daily lives. It is no coincidence that Aphrodite was the wife of Hephaestus, the mythical master craftsman of jewelry befitting the gods. The implication in the myth, if viewed archetypally, is that craft needs beauty. It is beauty that craft strives for, so we see her importance in crafting the image. But it would be a mistake not to perceive that all the gods are involved in all our endeavors. There are other gods and goddesses at play in art-making and in therapy and education. There is bright-eyed Athene, goddess of invention and practical counseling, and Hermes with his mediating communication and helpful transitions, taking advantage of chance events.

There is a function represented by each archetype, but there is a necessity for love and beauty. If we would only spend as much time and energy teaching students and patients to see Aphrodite's goldenness in everyday objects and events—remembering the images of the soul—as we now spend teaching techniques, we would find more lively works of art and fewer lifeless academic works. We would also experience greater and deeper healing and education. Through psychological seeing and aesthetic perception the object becomes active. It is made pregnant. Then it produces and one's work becomes more vital. The very ground of the sensate world, its very existence, lies in the lap of this goddess of love and beauty.

Beauty is an ontological necessity grounding the sensate particularity. Without Aphrodite, the world of particulars becomes atomic particles. Life's detailed variety is called chaos, multiplicity, amorphous matter, statistical data. Such is the world of sense without Aphrodite. Then sense must be made of appearance by abstract philosophical means—which distorts philosophy itself from its true base.[7]

Personifying

Psychological seeing, then, is a form of aesthetic perception. It is seeing with the eyes of the soul, proceeding from personified figures in the heart rather than from mental concepts and techniques. Aesthetic perception needs aspiration and inspiration—a wonder which precedes intellectual wonder and inspires the given beyond itself, motivating the artist in each of us, letting each thing reveal its particular aspiration within a cosmic arrangement. Aesthetic breathing in the world is a form of taking it to heart, interiorizing it, hearing the world soul in the speech of things. "Taking in" means interiorizing the object into itself, into its image so that its imagination (rather than ours) is activated, so that it shows its heart and reveals its soul, becoming personified and thereby lovable.[8] The object's activated imagination shows the hand what needs to be done.

Personification is a structuring agent; it is "poiesis." It is helpful to see figures in a picture as complexes walking around and talking to each other rather than paying attention to our personal feelings. This is because personal feelings lead us away from the psychic drama. In our materialistic culture we no longer believe in imaginary persons who "could possibly be as they present themselves, as valid psychological subjects with wills and feelings like ours but not reducible to

---

[7] James Hillman, *The Thought of the Heart and The Soul of the World* (Dallas: Spring Publications, 1992), 45.

[8] *Ibid.*, 47-48

[9] James Hillman, *Re-Visioning Psychology* (New York: Harper & Row, 1997), 2.

ours"[9] Therapy—or soul-making—depends upon our ability to personify the movements of the soul in our daily experience, revivifying
our relations with the world we encounter and hearing the many voices
within each of us. Our goal is to acknowledge Psyche's needs and her
influence in our lives. For this "we need an imaginal ego that is at
home in the imaginal realm, an ego that can understand" the major
task now confronting psychology: differentiation of the imaginal; discovering its laws, configurations and moods of discourse, and its
psychological necessities. But this major psychological task of differentiating the imaginal begins only when we allow it to speak as it
appears—which is personified. Personifying is thus both a way of
psychological experience and a method for grasping and ordering that
experience.[10]

By achieving this psychological task, one's hand is given the means
of sure craft—skill in the perception of the essential reality we face.
It is the anima who teaches personifying, and who activates the hand
of the artist. Her very first lesson is the reality of her autonomous
personality, so difficult for us to accept in our common ego-centered
experience. Her second lesson is the necessity of love. Anima comes
to life through love, just as Psyche in the myth is mated with Eros,
who rescues her from her deathlike stupor.

With aesthetic perception we see personifying as a way of knowing and doing. It is a more subtle and sensitive way of apprehending
the world, giving things vitality and meaning. Personifying is a way of
seeing the world ensouled, independent from us, with its own inte-
rior existence and capable of experience, obliged to a history and
motivated by purpose and intention. A personified world implies a
passionate engagement with the things we perceive. This is the true
craft—skill in the perception of the independent subjectivity of the
things we encounter.

The older notion, that we develop skill by following directions
and learning predetermined techniques, derives from a belief in the
analytical concept that says we can understand anything by studying
its parts. Aesthetic perception does not respond in analytical terms
but rather requires that we face the world in its very presentation. It
is here in the face of the world, and in facing it, that authentic response

---

[10] *Ibid.*

is possible. It is here also where therapy occurs, for:

> Images are primordial, archetypal, in themselves ultimately
> real. They are the only direct reality that the psyche ever
> experiences. As such they are the shaped presences of ne-
> cessity. The image turns our "pathologizings" into inner
> archetypes, teachers, as they move from generalities and
> abstractions of conceptual cognition to the concrete im-
> mediacy and multivalence of events. [11]

It is not we who are the teachers and therapists. Rather it is the
inner archetypes who teach us to be true to our own natures. We do
not need prescribed techniques when we can converse with material
things by seeing them as psychic realities. We find the means at hand
to craft the image because the natural sanctity of things grips our
hearts and we can love the material shapes, colors, and rhythms of
our everyday world. Such a heartfelt relation with reality embodies
the necessary craft to give form to the image.

The importance of this attitude for art therapy should be stressed.
Craft is the artists' careful perception of—and attention to—the world
of their senses. The teacher or therapist will find their craft in careful
attention to the art work which the student or patient has produced
rather than to abstract concepts about the patient's past or the student's
academic prowess. Skill and technique are best when they come from
the drive to give a face to the invisible image and not from principles
gathered from other people's experiences and accomplishments. But
such an attitude is not simply given in our modern materialistic world.
It is not a spontaneous reaction. Rather it must be provoked, called
forth, "raged," as Hillman puts it, "or outraged" into life. Leaving
these forces unprovoked could be detrimental. "What is passive, immobile, asleep in the heart creates a desert."[12]

The discipline required for such efforts is much greater than that
required of an academic art education with its rules and principles.
Without the manifestation of the image the work will be lifeless. Such
exactness (the anxiety of a Cezanne, the desperation of a de Kooning)
requires real passion. It may even need outrage at the aridity of academic and scientific expectations—a rage that can tear one away from

---

[11] *Ibid.*, 64.
[12] *Ibid.*

the safety of convention and generality. Yet it does no good to denounce the academic language of technique and power if we can suggest no way to promote genuinely imaginal artistic achievement.

Once a fourth grade boy came up to my desk to ask how to draw a hand. My response was not what the boy expected: "A hand? A hand? There is no such thing as "a hand." What do you mean?" I said. Growing a little frustrated the boy replied, "How do you draw a hand? You know, a hand," and he shook his hand in my face.

"Oh," I said as if suddenly understanding, "an angry hand shaken in someone's face." "No," he said. "I want to draw a hand holding a baseball bat." He had already been provoked, even outraged, so now I could help him to get in touch with the image he was trying to depict. I began by asking him about the game. "You like to play? Are you good at it?" I asked. "Oh yes, I'm the pitcher for our team." And thus began a discussion about how he holds the baseball bat differently during a game when the bases are loaded than when he is in practice. "Oh, I get it.," he said and went back to his table.

Later he came to me smiling and proudly holding the drawing up for me to see. This drawing had more authority and genuineness than might have come from a lesson in how to draw "a hand." It required a new step in the traditional process. There are no traditional techniques for saying what the student wanted to say. Technique alone can only produce lifeless forms. A prescribed technique for drawing a hand already shapes the "a hand" before it is fully experienced in the present moment. Actually, "a hand" cannot be experienced; it is a mere generalization (**figs. 21-23**).

Once one is in touch with the enchantment of the image, fingers will know what to do. They will be directed by the complexes, one's pathologies, and one's inner archetypal teacher, who appear in the half-light of negative capability. They do their finger-work in the primal clay of the imagination which is fed by experience. In a moment of vision, an object or experience is illuminated with significance.

Although craft does require constant attention and ritual, it is not mere practice to gain facility in the use of tools or knowledge about the traditional way things are formed. Rather it is related to the ideas we gain from intense experience, the images we gain through aesthetic perception. The Greek word for craft was *techne*, but as

Heidegger makes clear, *techne* belongs to "bringing forth," to poiesis. "It is something poetic... It reveals whatever does not bring itself forth and does not yet lie before us."[13] The challenge was to get this fourth grader to see his task more as "bringing something forth" (his image of the game) rather than as representing a literal generality. I tried to provoke the heart, and his heart was truly in the game, but obviously not yet in the drawing. This did not occur until he became vaguely aware of involuntary memory (*memoria*).

Myth and Memory

Identification of present with past is the essence of myth—*mythos* and *memoria*—because they are of the timeless world of the psyche. Myth is the telling word, not just any word, but that word which matters, the essential, the extratemporal. Here the story each object or event has to tell as it presents itself to the heart is important. "For Mythos is what gives form and style and makes us conscious of the process; through mythos we can describe life in a coherent way"[14]

In the language of archetypal psychology, the fourth grader, through his drawing, was in touch with the archetypal hero—batting a home run. Even if the drawing was somewhat crude and unskilled, the drawing was more powerful than other work that may have been more technically competent. Teaching situations which provoke the sleeping hearts of the students do promote craftsmanship. Telling is important. To tell is to lay bare. The drawing of a child batting a ball reveals a vital image and has a psychologically healing effect. "To the extent that I managed to translate the emotions into images—that is to say, to find the images which were concealed in the emotions—I was inwardly calmed and reassured," Jung wrote in his autobiographical work, *Memories, Dreams, Reflections*.[15] The craft in therapy is to translate the emotions into images.

---

[13] Martin Heidegger, *The Question Concerning Technology and Other Essays*, William Lovit, trans. (New York: Harper & Row, 1977), 13.

[14] Michael Meade, "On Being a Man: An Interview With Michael Meade,"*The Santa Fe Sun* (Santa Fe, New Mexico, 19), 6.

[15] C. G. Jung, *Memories, Dreams, Reflections* (New York: Random House, Vintage Books, 1965), 177.

Archetypal themes—such as the fourth grade boy and the hero—stimulate personal complexes that animate the story of life and ordinary existence. We must acknowledge that each item of our personal experience is also archetypal. Robertson discovered that these themes provide invaluable structure in art therapy.

> Archetypal themes which belong equally to all ages, and, rooted in man's remote past, can yet emerge in contemporary images. While they can provide the excitement of exploration, of discovery, they also provide a point at which to rest: they bear within themselves such a wealth of ripe tradition from the past that even to sink into them empty or uninspired is to be borne up by rich and teeming associations. They offer, as it were, a vertical path back to the core of oneself rather than the horizontal extension of many school activities— no less, if no more, necessary."[16]

Spontaneity

Art educators and art therapists emphasize spontaneity in an attempt to avoid influencing the patient's or student's work or distorting the psychological message. This is the reason we so often merely accept whatever scribbles or stereotypes a student or patient may present. The only valid conclusion we can draw from such stereotypical work (i.e. a heart in two pieces with an arrow going through it, a hypodermic needle without a context) is that the artist has not thought carefully has not allowed the image into the work, but has accepted a superficial convention. The artist has not provoked the heart and is resisting authentic commitment. We owe it to our patients and students to tell them the truth when they are resisting authenticity and are offering only generalizations. They are negating their own creativity and for therapists or teachers to accept such generalization without comment is to do harm to both the patient or student and to themselves. They are encouraging the negation of creative imagination.

Spontaneity is not merely a natural gift, and just asking students or patients to draw or paint or model whatever they wish is not

---

[16] Seonaid M. Robertson, *Rosegarden and Labyrinth* (Dallas: Spring Publications, 1989), 89.

Our patients and students must be encouraged to see with the eyes of the soul and to think with the heart. The too speedy pace of modern society and our common use of the term "spontaneous" suggest merely impulsive and unconstrained, or "off hand" action taken without thought. However this word "spontaneous" has deeper and richer connotations. It comes from the root meaning to draw out or stretch, to span. Here we come to the ideas of stretching our vision, of drawing out the image, and of spanning the gap between dull and lifeless convention and the animated object. The root of the word spontaneous also suggests "span," "to spin," and thus the idea of spinning or weaving a story. To weave relates to the word "text," and therefore texture and context. Perception of the image means seeing its texture. The body, according to Patricia Berry of the image is "woven with patterns offering a finished and full context."[17]

Other connotations derived from early roots of "spontaneous" are related to "spider" and "web," and also "pend," "to hang," as well as "to append," and "ponder." We even find vestiges of *penia* (lack or poverty—not knowing) in this simple word. All these ideas must figure into the context of our thinking about spontaneity. Real spontaneity, then, implies stretching the heart toward the god in the things of everyday life, spanning the abyss which separates the visible from the invisible, weaving a web of relationship through pensive meditation. Even when one is not conscious of these many connotations, they are, nonetheless, alive in the word and in the collective unconscious and can be sought out. They echo in the word if we listen carefully.

Certainly teachers and therapists have a responsibility to seek such deeper possibilities in the words we often use so thoughtlessly. The term, "off hand" is a good example. Because "craft" requires the skill of the hands, an "off hand" depiction would lack craft—no matter how well the artist used "proper" perspective, proportions, design principles, and color harmony.

We must discourage merely vacuous impulsive art work or work based on conventional standards and rational concepts which result in cold mechanical products that mask the psychic situation in the soul of the patient or student. We often unknowingly discourage our

---

[17] Patricia Berry, "An Approach to the Dream," *Echo's Subtle Body: Contributions to an Archetypal Psychology* (Dallas: Spring Publications, 1982), 59.

patients and students to have authentic contact with their own psyches by insisting on techniques, the learning of which we mistakenly call craftsmanship. The genuine speech of soul is silenced and the so-called spontaneous language turns out not to be their own, so that when they speak, they say nothing. Such conventional or pictographic signs are totally inadequate for therapy and for learning. They tell us that the patient or student is not in touch with his or her psyche, or is resisting exposure of the heart's thought. It is our duty as teacher or therapist to let the artists know their work is valueless when they are not speaking from the heart. We need to help the artists to get in touch with their feelings and authentic responses to the world, to help them find a form adequate to craft their own images, not to teach them a form or to give them our image.

Too often therapists and teachers are unaware of how important it is to help the patient or student to look for the image. We are under the misconception that we must accept uncritically whatever the student or patient presents. Are we afraid the patient or student is not strong enough to face reality? We must realize that stereotypes do not help the person who uses them, and that to passively accept such shoddy thinking is actually harmful. We can only help the person recognize the feeble and inadequate nature of such unproductive figures by valuing what is genuine in the work. We can point to the authenticity of the emotion and focus on its—the emotion's—need to see and be seen, and urge the patient or student to accept his or her personal involvement in the situation.

Often clinical language only masks the face of the emotions which are visitations from another world, the underworld, the world of Hades, who offers us the power and riches (Pluto) and beauty of the invisible background of all life, as Hillman tells us.

> Art therapy asks of each emotional condition what the
> emotion itself wants. What are *its* features, *its* characteris-
> tics? What does it want, not only from me and with me,
> but what does *it all* want to do and say and show? How
> may I serve this divine influx so that the God in the desire
> is served by my movements, my colors and brushes, my
> words and voice?[18]

---

[18] James Hillman, *Emotion* (Evanston, Ill.: Northwestern UP, 1992), xii.

To move the heart toward the world shifts psychology and art away from conceiving itself as a science to imagining itself more like an aesthetic activity. If unconsciousness can be redefined as insensitivity and the unconscious as the an-aesthetic, then training for psychotherapy, art therapy, and art education requires sophistication of perception. Training will be based in the imaging, sensing heart: call it forth and educate it. Psychotherapy will study in its training programs the embodiment of the *anima mundi*, whether in language, in arts, myths, or rituals; attempting to train the eye and ear, nose and hand to sense truly, to make right moves, right reflexive acts, to craft well. "The invisible work of making soul will find its analog in the visibility of well-made things."[19]

---

[19] James Hillman, "Anima Mundi," *Spring 1982* (Dallas: Spring Publications, 1982), 83-84.

VI

STICK TO THE IMAGE

To judge is to form ideas correctly, and therefore also possibly incorrectly.

—*Martin Heidegger*

For Beauty, as we have seen, means the form of what is presented, that which is breathed in *aesthesis*, and by which the value of each particular thing strikes the heart, the organ of aesthetic perception, where judgments are heart-felt responses, not merely critical, mental reflections.

—*James Hillman*

Like a uroboric circle, the fifth principle, "stick to the image," brings us back, at least in part, to the first principle, "give form." If it is the image we are concerned with, and if image is the invisible idea which hides itself behind reality, then we are confronted with the question: Is it possible to base a program on the invisible idea which hides itself behind reality? How are we to make judgments on the basis of something so obscure? This is a problem of evaluation. When we activate imagination and allow it to materialize, we do have a sound basis for motivating aesthetic perception and encouraging individual creativity in art-making.

If to be correct an idea must conform to its object, and if to judge is to form ideas correctly then we must be cautious in our judgments. When we judge, our goal must be to maintain the direction toward the object. "But the maintenance of direction is constantly beset by the possibility that we do not attain the direction, or else we lose it. The idea does not thereby become undirected, but incorrect with reference to the object."[1]

Maintaining Direction toward the Image

Lack of coming to grips with the nature and necessity of objective evaluation are the two greatest causes of failure in the professions of art therapy and education. The failure is manifested in a superficial and mediocre performance. We leave the student or patient to stumble along without constructive comment, or to give up and simply to doodle or indulge in easy stereotype and convention. Such prosaic practice is the result of a general lethargy in our contemporary culture which, following Nietzsche, can be attributed to an existential fear in the face of the impossibility of achieving the ideal. Unconsciously we feel inadequate and deficient in connection with the imagination. We harbor a latent existential dread which nurtures fear of not measuring up to the expectations not only of our peers and ourselves, but of the expectations of our very vocation itself. We may be afraid of facing the expectations of our professions, or naively unaware that such expectations even exist.

The object in art is the image, not the thing we see but the luster of its unique being. The work of art presents the image to us. It is not itself the image. Thus evaluation or judgment helps maintain the direction toward the image—see the image as image and stick to it. This is no easy task. Direction, if found, is easily lost. The psychic image "cannot be seen clearly; it is not reached through ordinary sense perception; it is not understood by ordinary logic; it cannot be named."[2] No wonder we hesitate to make dogmatic proclamations. However objective judgment need not be dogmatic, literal, or binding. It is neither a decree nor an order. To judge may be to mediate, to conciliate, to surmise. It is a reckoning inference, an appraisal. Judgment of this sort is an evaluation with prudence and discernment at its core. It is an opinion, an estimation.

---

[1] Martin Heidegger, *What is Called Thinking?* Fred D. Wiek and J. Glenn Gray, trans. (New York: Harper & Row, 1968), 38-39.

[2] Samuel Beckett, in *Beckett and Myth: An Archetypal Approach* , by Mary A. Doll (Syracuse: Syracuse UP, 1988), 9.

Certainty itself would have countless limitations. Yet we must search for some means of achieving valid opinions regarding art and image. Therapists and educators in general are concerned with the psychic situation as a whole, but add art to the equation and the focus shifts to the psychic situation's incarnation in the image. Judgment, then, becomes an estimation of whether a healthy imagination has brought forth a complete image. Judgment becomes a form of communication: "A work of art is not an invitation to respond in any way whatsoever. It is, however, a call to the sharing of human values as these are expressed within the artistic communicative process."[3]

Aesthetic judgment is not simply intellectual judgment. Nor is it moral judgment. Moral and intellectual judgment often contradict each other. It is important for a therapist to be aware of these inner conflicts. For example, I know a woman whose aesthetic judgment of Rubens' sensuous nudes is perfectly adequate, yet she does not like Rubens' paintings because her moral judgment gets in the way. She thinks they are licentious and salacious. Her intellectual judgment is that such nude figures are valid subject matter and that sensuousness is an archetypal attribute of Aphrodite. Rubens evidently triggers a complex in her and, if she were a therapist or teacher, she should be conscious of such a complex and take it into account when doing image-work.

Archetypal psychology recognizes the form and the value of each particular thing as it strikes the heart—the organ of aesthetic perception—where "judgments are heartfelt responses." Only then is the heart held in a direction toward the image. A grateful and thoughtful heart—not just good heartedness—is a first step. Judgments are heartfelt concern for the image that is presented as it is presented. Thought is required as well as gratitude and memory. There is a responsibly inherent in this idea. More than simple ingenious innocence is called for. The heart gives itself in thought about all that concerns us in so far as we are human beings. Only with such heartfelt thought do we gain contact with what touches us and defines our nature—contact with the image.

---

[3] Eugene Kaelin, *Aesthetics for Art Educators* (New York. Teachers College Press, 1984), 78.

Criteria for Recognizing an Image

Imagistic perception does not merely see a uniqueness that is there. Rather perceiving in this way helps create uniqueness. Uniqueness is created by poieses-shaping images. The imagistic eye sees in shapes. The perception of uniqueness begins with the eye that sees imagistically.[4] This is where our evaluation is bidden. Our essential nature, "the soul's code," defines the image (the gathering of the constant intention of everything that the heart holds), that is, what touches us in the sense that it defines and determines our nature. Our psychic images do determine our destiny.

Only the image can tell us about itself. It is complete just as it presents itself. We can think of a work of art as a dream, a complete image with many component images, each of which can stand on their own as "images of the image." In this way, literature written within the field of archetypal psychology becomes useful in art therapy and education.

Patricia Berry in an article entitled "An Approach to the Dream"— one of the earliest and most essential essays on the nature of archetypal images—makes a clear distinction between imagination and visual perception. "A fantasy image is sensate though not perceptual: i.e. it has obvious sensual qualities— form, color, texture—but these do not derive from external objects"[5] The imaginal and visual modes rely upon distinctly different functions. The imaginal is aesthetic in as much as it presents the quality of a living experience in a perceptual context. With imagination any question of objective referent is irrelevant. This does not mean that the imagination is not real, but its reality does not come from its correspondence to something outer.

Images are sensate but their bodies are metaphorical. Images have texture—woven patterns—which offer finished and full contexts. Here it becomes clear that an image is not just anything we see or think, not just any perceivable fragment. To be an image an object requires a context, an emotional structure and value. Berry examines

---

[4] James Hillman, *Egalitarian Typologies Versus the Perception of the Unique* (Dallas: Spring Publications, 1986), 49.

[5] Patricia Berry, "An Approach to the Dream," *Echo's Subtle Body: Contributions to an Archetypal Psychology* (Dallas: Spring Publications, 1982), 57.

"with more exactitude" what she means by image and lists seven essential qualities of an image. They are, in brief form, as follows:[6]

Sensuality: Images have a metaphorical body. They are perceivable but not optical.

Texture: "The word 'text' is related to weave. So to be faithful to a text is to follow its weave."

Emotion: Emotional qualities "adhere or inhere to the image and may not be explicit at all...We cannot entertain any image in dreams or poetry or painting, without experiencing an emotional quality presented in the image itself."

Simultaneity: "No part precedes or causes another part, although all parts are involved with each other....no part occurs before or leads to any other part."

Intra-relations: All the images are part of the overall image, "so that no part can be selected out, or pitted against the other parts."

Value: "Some images seem more potent, more highly attractive than others... When the dream presents an image that goes against the way things are naturally, let's assume such images to be of high value because they are examples of the *opus contra naturam*." They are less likely to be ego oriented and thus more important to the psyche. They make a stronger statement by shocking us into paying attention.

Structure: "Significant structural relationships exist within and among images... In some varieties of structural thinking, form and matter, structure and content, can be separated; in imagistic thinking these pairs are one."

Berry's seven criteria for recognizing an image can help us to maintain the direction toward the image and to estimate whether an image has been embodied in a work of art.

Of course Berry is not the first to attempt to establish a definition for images. Poets and artists have grappled with the idea for decades, frequently concluding that images are much more than mere visual cues. For example Ezra Pound, the founder of the imagist movement

---

[6] *Ibid.*, 58-63. Berry analyses the kind of reality an image has on pages listing the seven qualities of sensuality, texture, emotion, simultaneity, intra-relatedness, value, and structure which are discussed here.

in poetry, defined images as "that which presents an intellectual and emotional complex in an instant of time." For Pound the image is more than an idea, it is a vortex or cluster of ideas endowed with energy. A vortex from which and through which and into which ideas are constantly rushing.[7] Although he uses a different language, when Pound speaks of a complex in an instant of time, he seems to mean what Berry means by simultaneity of the image. Its multiple facets comprise the whole.

It is not the image that we want to evaluate in art therapy or art education. The image is always complete and right. Rather it is whether an image has been embodied in a sensuous construct, and here Berry's seven qualities offer tangible help. They are, she says, "a kind of analysis of the image." It is the whole archetypal image, not its separate fragments, that is educational or therapeutic. Therefore we must be able to recognize when an image is complete because such images offer the fullest possible expression and therefore carry the greatest educational or therapeutic value.

Image Work

Having gained at least a bare outline analysis of the nature of the image, we are now in a position to take up the task of considering how the five basic principles can be addressed in image work. Berry's final quality, structure, relates directly to the first principle, "give form." Structure tells us how much attention the artists have given to the image, how willing they have been to struggle with and maintain contact with the image, giving the whole image a coherent structure. Only by giving structure—or body—to the image can we learn or heal. And this requires cautious judgment on the part of the artist and, of course, on the part of therapist and teacher.

Eugene Kaelin, in his book *Aesthetics for Art Educators*, offers three categories which can help us focus on the aesthetic aspect of the image: the sensuous surface, experiential depth, and total expressiveness (which results from various combinations of the first two.) These guidelines serve to help us avoid non-relevant—in this case moral or intellectual—aspects. He emphasizes the unique referents within the

---

[7] Ezra Pound, *Literary Essays*, T. S. Eliot, ed. (New York: New Directions, 1954), 3-4.

context of one's experience of judging works of art, asking that our appreciation of the work be based strictly on aesthetically relevant criteria. "Not any old preference will do."[8] When we move into discussion that claims everyone must be an artists, then we risk the claim that art is simply a matter of personal taste. "If I like it, it's art to me." But this would mean that art has no authority and that there are no valid criteria for aesthetic judgment.

   If patients and students need acceptance and sympathy, they also need some criteria for discerning when they fail to maintain direction toward the image. In addition teachers and therapists can—and must—judge whether an image has been depicted, and if it has not been depicted we must help the student or patient to see the image more clearly and with greater involvement. The structure of the work of art tells us whether an emotion has been held aesthetically within its images. A restricted imagination is indicated by excessive emotion, and the fundamental cure of a disordered emotion is the restoration of the imagination and especially the archetypal imagination. Therapists and teachers must be able to judge whether the structure presents a total expression.

   For example, pictures by children and untutored adults which use "m" shapes for birds indicate little concern on the part of the artist. Edith Kramer, in her book *Art as Therapy with Children*, lists five ways children may use art materials, and only one is complete enough for our therapeutic purposes: 1) precursory activities such as scribbling and smearing; 2) chaotic discharge such as spilling, splashing, and pounding, or destructive behavior leading to loss of control; 3) art in the service of defense, i.e., stereotyped repetition; copying, tracing, and banal conventional production; 4) pictographs which replace or supplement words; 5) and formed expression, or art in the full sense of the word. This includes the production of symbolic configurations that successfully serve both self-expression and communication.[9] It is only with this last activity that a true image is formed.

   An image stands by itself. It stakes a claim to the pictoral field by ordering it with its particular shape. It shapes or orders the elements of a pictorial field into a unique structure. The artist's pictoral field,

[8] Eugene Kaelin, *op. cit.*, 1984, 75

[9] Edith Kramer, *Art as Therapy with Children* (New York: Shocken Books, 1971), 47.

according to John F. A. Taylor, author of *Design and Expression in the Visual Arts*, "is not the space which he frames, but the space in which his title is established. His title is as valid as his capacity to govern the field he has chosen to set apart…"[10] In other words it is as valid as his capacity to give shape to the image. In the making of his work the artist orders the elements of a pictoral field, physically shapes them, according to the shape of the image he holds. His "title" is the artist's claim to authority. It is only as valid as his ability to give structure to the image which he holds in his heart, in his thought, remembering the image and giving thanks. An image is not set apart. Instead it sets itself apart and appeals to the artist's instinct. It is a self-contained and self-complete order, a complex idea, an image.

Everything within the field goes on at the same time. It has no sequence, only the elements and their interrelations. An image is filled with complexity and it defines its own field.

When evaluating how well the image is depicted, it is important to point out when the person is making a wrong move depicting an image. Perhaps the image is blocked from saying what it wants to say. Or perhaps the patient or student is not listening to the character, his feeling tone is off, or he has resorted to banal convention. When an art therapy student wants technical advice, how to paint "right,"—a bowl round, for example—a therapist might ask, "Do you trust the hand that cannot make it round? Isn't that a statement too?"

Trust the hand's ability. The hand is the place of the unconscious that the conscious mind cannot order to do what it wants. The orders from the conscious mind—let's call it "Headquarters"—are: "Paint a round bowl with the light coming off right there." The hand—the Private—will not do it. And the moment a therapist intercedes, trying to tell the hand how to do what the head says it should do, you are on the side of Headquarters. You are trying to get the Private back in line. In therapy and art education we must remain on the side of the Private.[11]

---

[10] John F. A. Taylor, *Design and Expression in the Visual Arts* (New York: Dover Publications, 1964), 10.

[11] James Hillman, from my notes taken at two unpublished lectures sponsored by the art therapy program at the University of New Mexico on October 12 and December 7, 1983.

The Private may be trying to break Headquarters' instructions, but this is no easy out, no slump toward lax craftsmanship. The Private is a thinking soldier in the service of the image. When one paints the picture, the image is in action. The image is already present in the activity of painting; it is a struggle with embodiment. This is also the point where the painter wrestles with the angel—the more than human. This is the point where the Private gets his hip broken because he could not do what Headquarters wanted. The painter feels defeated by the angel. But if the painter persists, it changes him. He becomes a different person, gets a new name—the name of his true self.

Complexes and Images

The image is the structure that holds all the complexes together, and education or therapy is the process of dealing with these complexes. Successful therapy or education would get all the complexes— the complete or archetypal image—depicted. Here we use the psychological term "complex," but image as it is used here is similar. According to Jung, a complex is an association of a group of elements that are held together by a single emotional tone— not a single emotion. There is nothing single about an image except its parts. The emotional tone holds the elements together aesthetically in a unified structure, which will be visible in the work of art.

There is a certain inflation in talking about images. Thus to equate image with complex is to rub in a little salt. "It wounds the inflation and keeps the image close to one's own awareness and one's own pathologies so that the dark eye is looking as well as the bright eye."[12] But we must not get literal about what the image is. If we realize that what we see in an image are persons—complexes—walking around and talking to each other, we may realize that the image is less personally ours. Instead it consists of autonomous psychic personages. A move toward personal feelings and away from the image actually presented is a weak defense against our own ignorance—we do not know what to do with what is simply there.

There is something more than human in an image. It is like an angel— a messenger saying something, meaning something, moving

---

[12] Hillman's lecture, *op. cit.*

us. Angels are also full of violence and power and excitement. When dealing with energy that we do not quite understand, we tend to employ the Herculean ego, to analyze and thus to kill. That is not the way to evaluate the artwork of our students or patients. Rather than taking a scientific rational view, equating the image with a field of energy, or with the subject matter as such, see the image as the voice of the necessary angel of earth. He may not speak our language, but he lets us know what he is telling us, sometimes most effectively through poetry:

> Yet I am the necessary angel of earth,
> Since, in my sight, you see the earth again,
> Cleared of its stiff and stubborn, man-locked set
> And in my hearing, you hear its tragic drone,
> Rise liquidly in liquid lingerings,
> Like watery words awash; like meanings said
> By repetitions of half-meanings. Am I not,
> Myself, only half of a figure of a sort,
> A figure half seen, or seen for a moment, a man
> Of mind, an apparition appareled in
> Apparels of such lightest look that a turn
> Of my shoulder and quickly, too quickly, I am gone?[13]

How to Begin

It is our duty as teachers and therapists to do something, to respond to the image. We must be able to appraise its success, but it is best not to start by talking "about" the picture. Its message is expressed far better in its presence than we could ever say it. Instead start with a full respect for what has been done. Otherwise you are jumping over into something else—diagnosis, analysis—and denying what is there because you do not understand it. Keep looking at the picture as you would in an art gallery. You and the artist may want to share your responses to the picture, but it would be a mistake to think that the artist knows exactly what has been expressed. Artists know what their ego intention was, but they may not know what the psyche had in mind. As therapists or teachers our task is to help the artist

[13] Wallace Stevens, "Angel Surrounded by Paysans," *The Palm at the End of the Mind: Wallace Stevens Selected Poems and a Play*, Holly Stevens, ed. (New York, Vintage Books, 1973), 354.

learn to "read" the voice of psyche, to "hear" the image.

It is crucial to let the picture just "be." While you and the painter look at it and see what the picture starts to do to you, you might simply express a reaction without reading anything into it, just as you would react to a person you meet. For example, we often smile at a person we like or move away from someone who intimidates us. Keep the reactions to simple statements: we cut ourselves off from reactions by asking questions too soon. While it is not helpful to start off with judgment, you do need to ascertain the value of the work. Your immediate response is a kind of gut liking or disliking, so look again. This is not as easy as it sounds.

Art educators and art therapists are often afraid of doing harm if they do not accept everything presented by the patient or student as valid—even stereotypes and conventional symbols. (For example a heart in two pieces pierced by an arrow does not get in touch with an image, for each heartbreak is unique.) The teacher or therapist can go wrong in two ways: the way of the Great Mother, who accepts everything, or the way of the Great Father, who continually passes judgment and creates unattainable expectations. Both are traps intended to release an archetypal tension. Instead we must maintain the tension, both authenticate and judge. The tension is seen in the image of the two hands of God— mercy and judgment—and there is no way out of it. That tension is there all the time.

The therapist or educator's role is to keep the activity going by not interfering too much and yet keeping the patient or student in touch with the image. The first step is to realize that the psyche is ninety percent below the surface. Our main concern is neither with symbol nor image, but with the unknown which always carries a certain amount of fear. That sense of awe is crucial, and the anxiety one senses in the work is important. The image presents a complex idea, unknown and unknowable because of its infinite multiplicity. In the language of archetypal psychology, it works through repercussion or echo.

If you can get at the "little mechanisms," the image will take care of itself. Hillman, who emphasizes the importance of images in psychotherapy and dream work, suggests practical moves, or "gadgets," to help see how little mechanisms work in the image. Once we have seen the work of art as an image because it has a specific context, mood, and scene, we want to stick to it. This means to leave it in its precise presentation rather than begin to interpret it. We begin by describing it in detail. What is its mood? In what context are the parts of the image displayed? In what setting does the story take place? Consider every aspect of the picture and its relations with all the other parts to constitute the entire or essential image. A complete image can never be stated in a trivial manner. It must be embodied in a proper style or genre. Style is what makes things matter. A gay and frivolous mood would not be painted in dark and ominous colors, for example. The vehicle must carry the symbol—the shapes, colors and style must evoke the same image as the subject matter. This is especially important for evaluation. The painting is the object from whose face we read the image.

The following are "gadgets" delineated in several important articles on dream images written by Hillman. This assumes that dream images and artistic images can be viewed as analogous. Clearly there is a parallel between the two when, as Hillman writes, "an image perceived as a picture can tend to become optical and intellectual and distanced... But imagined as a scene I can get into it, and when imagined as a mood, it gets into me."[14] The same can be said about a picture seen as a picture, "but when seen as an image, a scene, or a mood, as a form or shape, or a face," we can get at the soul of the image.

Analogy: We ask "what is it like?" The figure in Munch's "The Scream" is to me like the sinking feeling I got when I was afraid I would flunk my graduate orals. It is like the whole world is falling out from under me and there is nowhere to turn. A pretty landscape painting may be like the song of a bird, or as delicate as a butterfly soaring on a gentle breeze. Harsh or muddy colors may be like the stomach flu, a sharp piercing pain, or the cracking of a bone. "If the analogizing process goes on long and deeply enough, the truths that come are many, are radical, and are always relative to the dreamer's [or artist's]

---

[14] James Hillman, "Further Notes On Image," Spring 1978 (Dallas: Spring Publications, 1978), 159. In *Spring* 1977, 1978, and 1979 Hillman published his three definitive essays on image, "An Inquiry into Image," "Further Notes on Image," and "Image Sense." These essays are basic to understanding archetypal psychology's concept of image and image-work.

[15] *Ibid.*, 158.

images."[15] A radical or unexpected image is judged to be especially valuable: "The dream [picture] is the teacher in analogy; it keeps us in the functional operation of the image itself while enlarging it's meta-phorical body."[16]

Restatement: Reiterating the parts of the dream [picture] like a ritual chant "serves [the image] best because the image is usually not full enough to our untrained ears that miss the undertones and overtones. We must recognize our native weakness here. Our eyes lack the train-ing needed to read the image, and our ears to hear it. Restatement also synchronistically relates the dream [picture] to many parts of that larger image which is [the patient's] life."[17]

Simultaneity: Using "when/then" is a way of recognizing the si-multaneity of the parts of the image Since the elements in a picture are all there before us at the same time, no matter which was drawn first or which last, the image is presented all at once. As all the parts of the image are interrelated, we can emphasize their simultaneity: when "this" happens in the image then "that" happens.

Eternalizing: An even stronger statement can be made by eternalizing the image. Whenever I come home the shepherd is small and isolated on the rocky brown mountain. "Whenever the water trough is full, the shepherd is on the arid mountain where a cactus grows." As we go through these chants, the small distant shepherd may resonate with various aspects of the patient's life, or riding home may seem relevant, or water trough, or being blue as I ride home. By these many restatements (and in actual practice there would be many more) the image is given volume and value.

Modifying parts of speech: Operational gadgets which help to break the usual conceptual way of thinking and thereby enrich the image, include modifying the parts of speech—nouns with adjectives, for example. Thus we are free to move from logical grammar and syntax to a poetic or psychological language. We might speak of the railed bridge in the Munch lithograph, or the blocked bridge, or the long narrow bridge. We may also modify the verbs. The figure is scream-ing desperately, or is frantically screaming, grievously screaming. It is

---

[16] James HIllman, "An Inquiry into Image," *op. cit.*, 87.

[17] James Hillman, "Further Notes on Image," *op. cit.*, 157.

a dire scream, a dangling scream. We may reverse the parts of speech. One's franticness is a screaming franticness, one's gravity is screaming, your narrowness is bridged, or you suffer a bridged block, or your blockedness bridges, you dangle screamingly.

Noting the prepositions: "Each preposition presents a different proposition."[18] Prepositions help determine the mood, scene, and context. They differentiate relations between figures. For example a man in an image is on a horse. He could be behind the horse or in front, leading the horse, or even under a fallen horse. One could run with a horse, or run away from it or toward it. The preposition changes the message in the image and illustrates the importance of sticking to the image.

Eliminating the punctuation: Another constraint of logical grammar is punctuation. If we remove the punctuation we may find startling ramifications because the usual rhythm, syntax, and emphasis become disorganized. Images tend not to follow rules of grammar. In description language changes.

Noting the hiatus: The disjunction or hiatus which brings internal tension to the image are helpful signals. Terms like "but," "suddenly," and "when," signal a rupture. "Everything seems pleasant *but* there is a hidden trap." Things were going fine when *suddenly* the cart turned over." "In the dream it seemed to be my mother *but* it really wasn't she."

Holding: Simply holding the image, keeping it, carrying it around with you is a mode of meditation or brooding. This is not to merely tote the image like a bundle. Rather it implies an intense burning concern held carefully in one's hands, mind and heart. Sticking to the image means loving the image. When we see the objects and events of this world as images, we cannot help loving them. Even the suffering of war—think of Picasso's "Guernica"—can fill us with a love for living.

Power in the Image

In therapy sessions we can never have a dream directly before us. Dream work is always done with the patient's report of the dream. In art therapy we also work with the verbal assessment of the picture

---

[18] *Ibid.*, 134.

by both patient and therapist, but the actual concrete picture is there before us as we work. This can be an advantage but it may also be a disadvantage. One advantage is that it helps us to stick to the image: the picture is right there before our eyes. A disadvantage is that we sometimes begin to take the picture as the object of our quest rather than reading it metaphorically as a fantasy image. The naïve patient is likely to read the picture literally: "This is my house with the barn and water trough and the shepherd across the fence on the mountains. I am coming home on my horse after riding the range." Read as image, the picture offers multiple possibilities, more each time we go back to it.

This is not to say that every image created by a patient will have such powerful qualities. Like dreams, we instinctively know which are powerful and which are more banal. Kramer says it is in the skill of a therapist to spot when an image has potential for therapy and when one may be less useful. The art therapist:

> distinguishes work that is predominately formless and cha-
> otic; art that is conventional and stereotyped; pictographic
> communications that can be understood only if the painter
> explains their meaning; and complex aesthetically valid cre-
> ations that possess to a greater or lesser degree the qualities
> which we associate intuitively with art in the full sense of
> the word.[19]

When a valid image is presented, the challenge is to maintain the precision by reading and rereading the image, hearing and rehearing, chanting the elements of the image and their interrelations in a kind of ritual fashion. Restating the image close to its own speech, letting it speak in multiple restatements, gives rise to more possibilities for connections to appear and psychic patterns to emerge. "Restatement serves it best because the image is usually not full enough to our untrained ears that miss undertones and overtones."[20] Restatement also relates the image to the many parts of the student's or patient's life. As we go through this chanting, this singing the verses of an image as if it were a round or fugue, a deeper significance begins to resonate, giving more and more possibility for connections to appear and psychic patterns to emerge.

[19] Edith Kramer, *Art as Therapy with Children* (New York: Shocken Books, 1971), 3.
[20] James Hillman, "Further Notes On Image," *op cit.*, 157.

Each image has a specific context, mood and scene. Perhaps our first response to an image is to its mood—it is a sad picture, a depressing or an exciting one, or perhaps it is calm and pleasing. The mood will become more specific when the context in noted since the context is largely responsible for the mood. In the example of Munch's "The Scream," the context is a lonely, fragile, screaming figure from whom society is gradually receding—the two figures at the far end of the bridge, the lake with its ships, and finally the village which has become cloud-like and indistinct. Notice how the image works, its actual qualities, the parts considered in relation to the others. Multiple implications—circular reiteration—emerge through a precise portrayal of the pattern. "The subliminal richness is another way of speaking of the picture's invisible depth, like Pluto is another way of speaking about Hades."[21]

The hidden connections are already there in the person of the artist even before he or she created the picture. That is why in therapy we do image-work to seek out these connections operationally. This operation is a matter of word play. It is "a way of talking with the image and letting it talk." As we play with the image, "We watch its behavior—how the image behaves within itself. We watch its ecology — how it interconnects' by analogies, in the fields of my life."[22]

The purpose of working with images is to make them matter. By careful analysis we may disclose the multiple connections. Thus the image takes on weight and can even make us feel that we are walking on its ground, seeing ourselves reflected within the image.

When looking at dreams as images, "we have to look at the dream's words doubly carefully, because there is nowhere else to look."[23] However with a picture we do have somewhere else to look, and we are tempted to see the picture as a concrete object and not as an image, leading us to miss the image for the sake of the material object and literal content. It becomes psychologically significant only when we see it as an image. A poetic understanding does not consider an image as a message or as information about something other than itself.

---

[21] James Hillman, "An Inquiry into Image," Spring 1977 (Dallas: Spring Publications), 80.

[22] *Ibid.*, 81.

[23] James Hillman, "Further Notes On Image," *op cit.*, 170

The image is the formal cause, giving shape, color, and mood to any experience. Painted images can be experienced without reference to the object painted. And they do not refer to an invisible essence of the model, although they may be analogous to that essence. The image transcends such referent evocations. "An image is not an image *of* an object. It images itself. Thus whatever the image imagines are now 'imaginal parts' of the image." If we are to speak of the image and let it speak to us, then, as Hillman says, at least two senses are needed to grasp it. "We listen to the dream to see what it is telling us… We see through our hearing and listen into our seeing."[24] The painted image is aesthetic because it is perceived. It presents the object as it shows itself in all the radiance of its being. Psyche is located in the painted image. The artist does not paint for the sake of art but rather to give form to the image and to realize its beauty.

Once again we can turn to poetic language to see how contact with past joy or trauma can be therapeutic. Beckett calls imagination "involuntary memory," which can unite subject and object, "in a timeless union by restoring the past in all its sensuous and emotive totality." We may misperceive the image and see it unimaginatively. But seeing it imaginatively through "involuntary memory" constitutes a reduplication, making the experience "at once imaginative and empirical, at once an evocation and a direct perception, real without being merely actual, ideal without being merely abstract, the ideal real, the extratemporal."[25] This is the profound experience of imagination.

What do we actually evaluate when we look at a picture? First we are moved by it. What does not move us is considered worthless. We may be moved because a picture pleases us and brings us joy, or we may be moved if it displeases us. It may make us angry or it may make us sad. A picture might be depressing. These and the whole range of emotions may be evoked by pictures. But we must be careful to notice if it is the picture itself that moves us, or if it is some concept which we read into the picture.

There is no mathematical measurement for involvement, just as there are no techniques for depicting the image There can be no scientific or mechanical measurement for evaluating works of art. The

---

[24] James Hillman, "Image Sense," *op. cit.*, 130.
[25] Samuel Beckett, *Proust* (New York: Grove Press, 1931), 54-56.

special value of an archetypal approach is that it proceeds from the literal to the metaphorical. If art therapy and art education were based on Archetypal ideas, these professions could carry imagination into our culture at the grass roots level. Archetypal psychology, recognizes the authority of art and the autonomy of the psychic image. It is the only psychology to offer an aesthetic foundation for the professions of art education and art therapy.

In education as well as in therapy we are concerned with psychological and aesthetic integrity rather than egotistical gratification. Yet every object contains anomalies and contradictions. The image consists of endless variations that shift the foundation beneath the viewer so that no single position or mind set can serve as guide post. "A psychic substance does not and cannot mean one thing."[26] It is not a reflection of an external object but, as Jung insists, it is a fantasy figure. "It represents an inner reality which often far outweighs the importance of external reality.... The image is a condensed expression of the psychic situation as a whole..."[27] This is what gives art its significance in therapy and in education.

In our disordered world, art education and art therapy have an authenticity often missing from daily life. And it is through images and our association with them that we gain authority in a world dominated by scientific and rational thought. This is our aesthetic claim to healing:

> For when an emotion is not held aesthetically within its images— when the images have been reduced in quality, captured by collective consumerism, harnessed to political exploitation, voided by rationalism—then emotion runs rampant and we have to damp it down with drugs or exorcise it through therapies of release and expression. Instead I am suggesting that restoration of imagination is the fundamental care of disordered emotion, and especially the imagination that welcomes and gives place to the more than human.[28]

---

[26] James Hillman, "Salt: A Chapter in Alchemical Psychology," *Salt and the Alchemical Soul* (Woodstock, Conn.: Spring Publications, 1995), 149.

[27] C. G. Jung, *Psychological Types*, *CW 6* (Princeton: Princeton UP, Bollingen Series, XX, 1971), § 743 and 475.

[28] James Hillman, *Emotion: A Comprehensive Phenomenology of Theories and Their Meanings for Therapy* (Evanston, Ill.: Northwestern UP, 1992), xv.

Relevant Titles from Spring Publications

Working with Images: EDITED BY BENJAMIN SELLS
The Theoretical Base of Archetypal Psychology

The theory and practice of archetypal psychology is here set forth by some of its pioneers. Included are James Hillman's classic papers, "Archetypal Psychology: Monotheistic or Polytheistic," "Peaks and Vales," and "Image-Sense," as well as essays by Henry Corbin, Thomas Moore, Patricia Berry, Mary Watkins, and Wolfgang Giegerich. *Working with Images* is indispensable for grasping the radical thinking of Jungian imaginative psychology. Sells's introductions clarify the place of each work in the whole. (216 pp.) ISBN 0-88214-376-X

Imagination is Reality   ROBERT AVENS

Imagination is Reality is the first comprehensive essay to place Archetypal Psychology within modern thought, the tradition of mythical thinking, and to recognize imagination as the primal force of human life. By drawing upon four twentieth-century thinkers—Jung, Cassirer, Barfield and Hillman—Robert Avens clarifies the post-Jungian direction of psychology as it moves towards poetic and polytheistic imagination. Avens's easy familiarity with his subjects and startling insights make this book an introductory text and an advance into new territory. (128 pp.) ISBN 0-88214-311-5

The Cult of Childhood   GEORGE BOAS

Could our fascination with our early years and the issues of child abuse, abortion, and family therapy mean that we are caught in a myth of ideal purity and innocence? Innocence, rather than the true nature of children, may be a fond fantasy about them. By examining the idea of childhood, Boas exposes the buried assumptions that continue to influence nearly everything we do and say about children. (120 pp.) ISBN 0-88214-218-6

Rosegarden and Labyrinth   SEONAID M. ROBERTSON

A classic work in art education by one of the field's most thoughtful practitioners. With care and precision Seonaid Robertson explores the relationship between art and psyche. Focusing on the drawings of children and adolescents, she views these first products of the imagination against the backdrop of artistic and cultural history. Illustrations, index. (xxix, 216 pp.) ISBN 0-88214-319-0

SPRING PUBLICATIONS, 28 FRONT ST., SUITE 3, PUTNAM, CT 06260
TEL 860 963-1191   FAX 860 963-1826

DATE DUE